PASS THE BOOK
Read It - Sign It - Give it to a Friend

Tell us where you read the book
and enter the Hall of Fame.
Share a Story
andrea@andreacostantine.com

connected

101 WAYS TO BE OF SERVICE AND CREATE COMMUNITY

ANDREA M. COSTANTINE

Connected: 101 Ways to Be of Service and Create Community

Copyright © 2012 by Courageous Living, LLC

All rights reserved. This book, or parts thereof, may not be used or reproduced in any form without permission by Courageous Living, LLC

Book Cover: John Driscoll, J Driscoll Designs
Editing by: Donna Mazzitelli, Writing with Donna
Layout/Design: Andrea Costantine
Author Photograph by David Weihnacht, David Marc Photo

Printed in the United States of America

First Edition
ISBN 978-0-615-64743-2

Dedicated to my partner,
Roberto. Your endless love and
support keep me going.

This book is broken down into various sections in which you can GET AND STAY *Connected*.

Use this book...
- For inspiration and initiation
  - To find opportunities to connect
  - For new ideas to serve and create community
  - To remember how you can make a difference

Read *Connected* from COVER TO COVER or flip through and see what page is calling to YOU.

Happy COMMUNITY making!

introduction

Connected isn't about technology, computers or keeping "**in the know**" through social media or the online news channels. The connection I speak about in this book represents *our link to humanity—who we are as people and how we are all truly interconnected*. It is about **stepping away from a "me-focused" agenda** and shifting towards a **"we-focused" world**. A WORLD IN WHICH WE COLLABORATE, SHARE RESOURCES, CONNECT AND THRIVE. A world in which we look out for our neighbors, make choices that impact the whole—not just our own livelihood—for the greater good. A world in which compassion, love and empathy lead and peace prevails.

Connected is the start to seeing and being a different kind of human being. One in which we take **conscious actions, contribute to humanity** on a soul level—without the need for anything in return—to **be of service and unite** people merely for the sake of bringing people together and doing good.

What if we lived in a world where every single person mattered? What if we all knew and felt that WE BELONG, that NONE of us ARE SEPARATE or disconnected and that we all have a beautiful,

MEANINGFUL PLACE IN OUR SOCIETY and the world? What if…

This is what being connected means. It is **action that helps us all see and believe that we matter—that we are not alone—and more importantly, that we can make a difference.** Every single person can make a difference, regardless of your race, color, religion, wealth or any other factor. We can. But MAKING A DIFFERENCE ALWAYS BEGINS WITH US.

> *"I always wondered why somebody doesn't do something about that. Then I realized I was somebody."*
> - Lily Tomlin

Creating a different world starts within and moves outside of us. It starts with *one small change* in how we interact with people. **It's compassion. It's mindfulness. It's patience.**

I believe that all human beings need to know they matter, that they belong and they can make a difference. When we start to realize these three things—that we matter, we belong and we can make a difference—**we pass that empowerment on to others.** And ONE by ONE, the world becomes a better place. *The more we give of ourselves in the spirit of service, the more we are all connected and united.*

Throughout my life I've felt called to serve, but it wasn't until recently that I CONNECTED with ways to be of service that are in complete alignment with my vision. Today, **I joyfully seek to inspire others to create a sense of community through contribution, compassion and connection.** I know that for each person who adopts the spirit of service in their world, amazing things begin to happen. No longer is the world a mean and cruel place. It becomes a place of compassion, empathy, empowerment and connectedness. IT IS MY VISION TO SEE PEOPLE UNITE. It is my vision that we recreate a world in which resources are shared and plentiful. It is my vision that any **illusions of disconnection, loneliness and unimportance diminish** with each act of service and community-building we make. It is also my vision that every person on this planet feels as though they belong—that they matter and can make a difference. EACH AND EVERY PERSON HAS A SPECIAL PLACE HERE ON OUR PLANET. **When we honor our own divinity, we then honor it in everyone around us.**

We all have the power to make a difference in this world. Each action we take and each thought we think impacts others. Every act and every thought becomes a **ripple** that is sent out into the energy of those around us—**creating change one person at a time.**

I must disclose that being in a place of service is not about sacrificing your own life and well-being for that of those around you. It is, however, about SMALL LOVING INTERACTIONS THAT HEAL AND UNITE PEOPLE. It is about seeing an opportunity to serve and seizing it. It is not about doing it all alone, becoming a martyr or resenting the ways in which you selflessly give to others. It is simply about finding ways to *bring people together* and creating a sense of *belonging* that *reverberates* through our *communities*.

The 101 ways that are listed in this book are meant to spark your inspiration. They are not meant to be restrictive or a culmination of all that's possible. You can use this book in whatever way works for you, whether you **grab a handful of ideas** and repeat them or use it as a tool in which you seek new ways to be of service. I continue to put these into practice as often and as much as I can, although I have not yet completed every one. I may never. But I offer them as a **gift to expand upon.** Take these ideas and make them your own. Whatever you do, however, just don't keep them to yourself.

I bring this book to you with great love and compassion, and I hope one day we will meet in person and celebrate our unique CONNECTEDNESS and **passion for service.**

In Loving Service,
Andrea Marie Costantine

neighborhoods

neighborhoods

neighborhoods

neighborhoods

Our neighborhoods give us a multitude of ways to be connected and of service, yet **how often do we pass the people we live by without a second thought?**

When I purchased my first home in a suburb of Orlando, Florida, I was greeted with friendly neighbors. One neighbor delivered homemade cookies to my door and shared the history of my new house with me. I learned all about the people who had lived there before me, including what changes and updates they'd made to the house and what was original. In that neighborhood, **people looked out for each other.** There was an evident **sense of community.** From block parties, to social gatherings, these people knew how to be connected and create community.

LOOK for an opportunity to serve.

Shovel your neighbor's sidewalk after a snowfall or dust the snow off their car.

It's a special treat to receive such a random gift. Whenever you see the opportunity, notice what you can do for your neighbor.

This year we've had a lot of snowfall in Colorado, and it seems like everyone chipped in to keep the sidewalks clean and clear of ice. On numerous occasions, we went outside and found our sidewalks already shoveled. We have repaid that kindness whenever we could to do the same for our neighbors.

One chilly day in Denver, when I was living with my sister, a neighbor cleaned the snow off my sister's car. When she went out to her car in the morning, she was thrilled. It's a wonderful feeling to know someone took a moment to stop and complete a simple act of service.

For you, perhaps a neighborly act doesn't include snowfall, but there are plenty of other opportunities to be of service to your fellow neighbors. Look for those occasions.

The duty of helping one's self in the highest sense involves the helping of one's neighbors.
— Samuel Smiles

Can you name

Grab your neighbor's newspaper or other packages when they are out of town and stow them away until they get back home. A stockpile of newspapers in the front yard is a telltale sign of an empty home, which makes it a prime target for unwanted visitors. Keep your neighborhood safe by not accidentally welcoming intruders.

your neighbors?

CREATE A NEIGHBORHOOD CONTACT LIST.

If you don't have a contact exchange already in place, take charge and create one. Knowing your neighbors' phone numbers and emails will not only help in an emergency, it also allows you to be more neighborly and proactive in building connections. We had a list like this when I lived in Florida and it came in handy more times than I could have imagined. You can also use this list to notify everyone when someone is in need, whether due to an emergency (fire, break-in, illness) or a celebration (anniversary, new baby).

Start a neighborhood watch.

While "neighborhood watch" programs don't seem to have the spark they did years ago, it's part of our responsibility as a neighbor to look out for one another. We all want other people to keep an eye out for our property and safety, so be sure to do the same for others. If you see anything suspicious, speak up.

I want you to be concerned about your next door neighbor. Do you know your next door neighbor?
- Mother Teresa

You can make a difference in someone else's life. A gesture BIG or SMALL goes a long way.

Plan a block party or spearhead an annual neighborhood event.

For a BLOCK party, invite everyone to come and hang out, bring a dish and mingle. Kids, dogs and family friends are all welcome. Better yet, get together for a cause or special event. Gather for a celebration—think Memorial Day or other holiday—or around a theme, such as to *collect supplies and donations for a neighbor going through a hard time.*

> Nothing makes you more tolerant of a neighbor's noisy party than being there.
> - Franklin P. Jones

If someone in your neighborhood has recently experienced a hardship—for example, a fire, burglary, other personal tragedy or illness—have everyone bring something to the gathering to contribute and offer as support. Families with special needs children or families facing illnesses can always use a little boost. A small effort will go a long way. **Look for opportunities to get together with your neighbors and lend a helping hand.**

You can also spearhead an annual neighborhood event. A chili cook-off, a summer BBQ, a Halloween block party or a holiday gala. GET CREATIVE AND MAKE YOUR OWN REASON TO CELEBRATE. Social get-togethers are a lot of fun and offer a great time for us to connect with those who live nearby. Rally your neighbors and find a common day, holiday or month where you can start a tradition of an annual neighborhood event.

Build a bonfire, light a fire pit and create a neighborhood drum circle.

Invite your neighbors for a night of fun. Host it in your backyard or take your get-together on the road (or to the woods). Kids love to play along when it comes to music and singing. Find the music gurus in your neighborhood, have them bring their guitars and look for other musical instruments, whether real or makeshift, to add to the circle. Music unites people.

During a recent birthday celebration, we all gathered around the fire pit in the backyard. With a few instruments, people began to sing along and found their own rhythm in the circle. It was a great evening and everyone felt connected and in sync with the rest of the group. (Of course, be sure your city or county allows bonfires before you start one! And find out if there is a cutoff time for extra outdoor "noise.")

Cheri Shanti has taken her passion for music and turned it into her vehicle for expression. Her work promotes Music Making, a powerful tool for community building in modern culture that helps individuals deal with depression and other symptoms of our modern times. In her book, *Muse Power*, she discusses the use of music making as a way to heal the self and sustain viable community. She also shares that music has many well-known and well-documented benefits for children including increased capacity for problem-solving, enhanced tolerance for diversity and global consciousness as well as a decreased sense of depression.

Music has always had a special place in my heart. Can you imagine a world in which we come together through the beat of connectedness?

We should learn to live and LOVE our neighbors as ourselves for the sake of PEACE and progress.
- David McCallum

Invite your neighbors over to your house for dinner, appetizers or game night.

Doing this is easy if you know how to get ahold of the people who live around you. **Make it a habit to get together—even if it's just once a year. Extend the invitation to** get to know your neighbors better. **Whether planned or a spur-of-the-moment event, seek out opportunities where you can learn more about the people who live in your** neighborhood.

My friend's neighborhood in Parker, Colorado has this idea down. Their neighborhood is especially friendly and community-oriented, **and they are known to hang out with one another frequently and enjoy everything from card nights to appetizers on the patio.**

SHARE RESOURCES.

HAVE YOU FOUND THE BEST

HOUSE CLEANER, GARDENER OR

HANDYMAN? WHY NOT LET YOUR

NEIGHBORS KNOW AND MAKE

THE INTRODUCTION AS WELL? WE

ALL LOVE TO GET CONNECTED

TO GREAT SERVICE PROFESSIONALS,

ESPECIALLY ONES THAT ARE LOCAL,

SMALL BUSINESS OWNERS. WHEN

YOU COME ACROSS THESE SUPERSTAR

PROFESSIONALS, PASS ALONG THEIR

INFORMATION AND SHARE THESE

VALUABLE RESOURCES WITH YOUR LOCAL NEIGHBORS. YOU NEVER KNOW WHEN YOU'LL NEED THE NAME OF A TRUSTWORTHY PROFESSIONAL, SO BE SURE TO START THE BALL ROLLING BY SHARING THE NAMES OF THOSE YOU RECOMMEND.

Host a Community Garage Sale.

Not only are community garage sales a great way to clean out your closets and clear out some unwanted items, but community garage sales attract a lot of attention from yard-sale avengers. Select a weekend, give everyone plenty of notice and set up shop. You can even rotate shifts with your neighbors to man the sale. Once the community sale is complete you can donate the rest of the items to a local charity. You could also donate all the proceeds to a local charity or a neighbor in need.

A fun way to raise money for charity is through your gently-used items. At a women's retreat I attend, we each bring nearly-new items to sell to each other. All the proceeds from the "bow-tique" are donated to the selected charity. It makes shopping fun and guilt-free.

Gather your gently-used goods and donate them to a local shelter. Whether extras from your recently-held garage sale or that extra juicer in the cabinet that's never seen its first fruit, put it to good use by passing it along. Coordinate a donation drop within the neighborhood by passing out fliers and letting people know where items will be picked up or how they can drop off their items at a designated spot. This will allow you to coordinate a larger donation to a local organization in need.

As we were putting the pieces of this book together, a large fire broke out in Jefferson County, Colorado. During that time a Facebook friend (Heather S.) wrote on her page: *"Starbucks donating coffee for the firefighters, four local restaurants banding together to feed all of them (around 500 now, I think), Anytime Fitness opening its shower facilities to the evacuated families, and so many area residents opening their homes to the evacuated so they don't feel quite so lost. This is a good place."* **This is what community is all about.**

At Work

If you work in an office, it's likely you spend more time with your co-workers than you do your family and loved ones. Within companies that cultivate a community feeling, individuals easily befriend their co-workers and feel as though they have a tight-knit family between the walls of their office. When you spend so much time with people, you can easily utilize these relationships for the benefit of all.

LIFT EACH OTHER UP.
WHEN IT COMES TO YOUR CO-WORKERS, REMEMBER YOU ARE PLAYING ON THE SAME TEAM. WHILE IT MIGHT NOT ALWAYS FEEL THAT WAY, YOU ARE. USE YOUR TIME WITH OTHERS TO BUILD THEM UP AND ENCOURAGE THEM TO GO FURTHER, PRESS HARDER AND REACH THEIR GOALS. FOR INSTANCE, USE HEALTHY COMPETITIONS SUCH AS WEIGHT LOSS GOALS OR GET TOGETHER TO VOLUNTEER AT A LOCAL CHARITY EVENT TO SUPPORT AND LIFT UP YOUR FELLOW CO-WORKERS.

I ONCE HEARD THAT THE **DEFINITION OF A HEALTHY RELATIONSHIP** IS WHEN THE *STRONGER PERSON* LIFTS THE OTHER PERSON UP TO THEIR LEVEL. A*N UNHEALTHY RELATIONSHIP IS WHEN THE STRONGER PERSON KEEPS THE OTHER PERSON DOWN.*
THINK ABOUT THIS IN ALL YOUR INTERACTIONS—**are you LIFTING people UP?** IF NOT, HOW CAN YOU START TO DO THAT? AT WORK, FOR EXAMPLE, YOU COULD TEACH A PERSON SOMETHING THEY DON'T YET KNOW, CREATE A MENTOR RELATIONSHIP OR INITIATE A HEALTH AND FITNESS CHALLENGE?

Be inclusive and

Work and school often create a breeding ground for isolation. IT'S EASY TO SLIP INTO A BELIEF THAT YOU DON'T BELONG. There was a recent commercial showcasing this fear. In the commercial, the co-workers sent out a text saying a taco cart had been set up in the break room. One person immediately felt they'd been excluded from the text, but in reality it was because their phone was too slow and the text had been delayed. It's a comical commercial, but the underlying truth is there—we all want to belong and feel included. If you work with someone who you haven't had the chance to get to know yet, invite them along on the next lunch outing.

Water cooler talk can be brutal, and you can expect the people you spend 40 hours a week with will sometimes push your buttons. That's natural. However, **don't instigate it by participating in office drama**. It'll likely happen, but as soon as you realize

speak kind words.

what's going on, see how you can redirect the conversation.

I like to do this by **complimenting the person being criticized or singled out**. Even if I agree with the water cooler talk, I don't want to participate in it. I'll usually say something like, "You might be right, but you know, Sally is really good at keeping everyone else in line." You'll notice WHEN YOU CHIME IN WITH A POSITIVE STATEMENT ABOUT SOMEONE, PEOPLE USUALLY FOLLOW SUIT. If they don't, walk away.

To take this one step further, don't be fooled into thinking that bullying is for kids. Workplace bullying is also quite prevalent in today's society. If you see someone constantly getting "picked last" at your office, what can you do to make a difference in that person's life? Underneath, we are all in need of love, companionship and connection.

THE TIME IS ALWAYS RIGHT TO DO WHAT IS RIGHT.
- Martin Luther King, Jr.

Offer support.

Your co-workers may need help outside the office. Perhaps they are dealing with family issues, ill health or a personal tragedy. While you never need to be a savior, do what you can to offer support when needed. It could be as simple as occasionally bringing lunch for someone or picking up a coffee for them on your way to work. We all want to know that people care about us. How can you make someone you work with feel special and important?

HOW CAN YOU OFFER SUPPORT?

_____

_____

_____

_____

_____

_____

Coordinate community involvement. Rally your co-workers and give back to the community. There are many options for group community involvement, from Habitat for Humanity, to adopting a road, to Big Brother Big Sister. Find a common cause that can gain support in your office and coordinate a giving back opportunity for all.

> Service to others is the rent you pay for your room here on earth.
> - Mohammed Ali

GET PHYSICAL. I'm in awe of companies that create a dynamic, collaborative working environment among their employees. **It takes time, attention and dedication from management to cultivate a culture of community.** Some companies go as far as to foster environments where their employees not only volunteer together, but they hike, road-bike and do other fun adventures that involve movement and getting physical.

Another great idea for companies is to host health challenges, encouraging employees to get together for workouts, to eat healthily and even lose weight. What could be better than losing weight at work!? If being physical doesn't work for you, why not get together in honor of your hobbies. Think guitar, cooking or even yoga.

Yum
Yum
Grub
Grub

Company Potlucks. Food brings people together. When under a tough deadline, or through a busy period at work, coordinate a potluck—or if you love to cook—go ahead and bring in food or a baked treat to share. If possible, get people to eat together too. Don't just dish out the food and send everyone back to their respective cubicles. Instead, encourage collaboration, connection and community through conversation. Besides, employees are more productive after taking a break. If you are planning a holiday potluck, contact your local rental company to bring in some extra chairs and tables so everyone can eat together.

Giveaway tables.

How many unwanted items do you have at home? Make a designated space or a table where employees can drop off unwanted items. Then, the other employees who are in need of something—say, a screwdriver or a baby item—can grab one from the table and take it home. What doesn't get picked up by another employee can be donated to Goodwill or another nonprofit that accepts used items. Clear up the giveaway table every quarter and encourage people to bring in additional items to be donated when it's nearing the donation drop-off time.

Make the choice to be your highest and best self, regardless of the circumstances.

- *Rosalene Glickman, Ph.D.*

Friends

Keep your life filled with true friends and loved ones. It is a guaranteed way to feel connected. The average person knows approximately 250 people. While this may sound like a lot, or even a little to some, friends are an integral part of our well-being. When we surround ourselves with loving, supportive people, our lives feel more full, rich and complete. Throughout my life, I've never had more friends than I do now. In just a matter of a few years, I developed a supportive network of friends and colleagues when I moved to Denver, Colorado. Perhaps this is one of the friendliest places on earth, but I think the truth is that so many of the people in this state are looking for and interested in building new relationships.

The saying, "to have a good friend you need to be a good friend," is one I believe in. If you'd like more friends in your life, look for ways to be a friend to the people you meet. Friendships take a little effort and persistence to start, but if you remain open, honest and loving in your encounters, you are sure to build friendships.

PRAY, send your friends love and keep them high in your thoughts. Our thoughts have an effect on others. When we think the best about people, we see the best in them. When we think the worst, we see their worst come out. People aren't perfect, and neither will your friendships be. Find a way to focus on what's right about the people in your life. This doesn't mean you should let people walk all over you, but this is about being of service. We serve no one by focusing on someone's weaknesses.

I've struggled with this myself. I am loving and compassionate, yet when I find a friend or loved one who doesn't want to put the energy and effort into changing, I get frustrated. I have to come back to the realization that I cannot change anyone, and at the end of the day all I can do is send them love. My loving thoughts will do more for them than anything else I might do. How can you lift your friends up?

Prayer is when you talk to God; meditation is when you listen to God.
~Diana Robinson

BE VULNERABLE AND AUTHENTIC. IT'S SCARY, BUT ALLOW YOURSELF TO OPEN UP. THE MORE WE OPEN UP TO OTHERS, THE MORE WE WILL RECEIVE OPENNESS IN RETURN. CAN YOU IMAGINE A WORLD WHERE OUR RELATIONSHIPS WITH OTHERS ARE PURE AND AUTHENTIC? WE'D ALL HAVE MUCH MORE LOVE AND COMPASSION TOWARDS EACH OTHER.

Many times we put up a front, act as if everything is okay and hide the truth of our feelings. Instead, why not share a piece of your truth with the people closest to you? They cannot offer back to you love and support if you don't give them the space to do so. And don't be afraid to admit your imperfections. People want to be friends with people they can trust. This includes someone who also makes mistakes.

Throughout the years I've had several people drop out of my life. I would email, call or reach out to them, but they suddenly stopped responding. This really disgruntled me. I couldn't understand what happened. Then one day, my own sister said my life seemed perfect to others. That's when it hit me. People perceived my "perfection" because I was putting out there a sense of perfection. Ironically, I'm not a supporter of perfection, so this was funny to me. Admittedly, I asked people about their lives more than I dished out the dirt of my own, which might have implied that things were all rosy in my life. This, however, wasn't the truth.

When I realized the assumptions made because of my behavior, it became a great opportunity for me to grow, to be more vulnerable and open with people and to share some of my struggles and challenges. I want to show that I, too, am just a human being. I constantly remind myself that we are all hurt little children living in adult bodies—we are all trying to find our way in the world. I am one of those adult children even if others don't perceive me that way.

WHAT ARE YOU PUTTING OUT THERE?

laughter is the shortest distance between two people.

Victor Borge

Laugh. I love laughing. What is better than a true, guttural **belly laugh**? Think of the times in your life when you LAUGHED SO HARD YOUR FACE HURT FROM SMILING, TEARS ROLLED DOWN YOUR CHEEKS and perhaps you even lost your breath. **When we laugh, we bond.** It may not be the easiest thing to plan, but we can all use more humor in our lives and not take this journey so seriously.

As a child, I loved to play practical jokes on my family members. My brother and I were notorious for setting up jokes on each other. One of my favorites was to tie a rubber band around the sprayer in the kitchen sink. When someone turned on the water quickly, water shot straight at the person standing at the sink. We'd always get a good laugh out of it—after the victim chased us around the house to get us back. I still love to pick up a fake spider or cockroach and place it in an inconspicuous place.

Lighten the mood with humor whenever you can. **Laughing is contagious.** Think about the funny laughs you've heard over the years—THE SNORTERS, THE SILENT LAUGHTERS, THE HYENAS. Try "pretend laughing" out loud now and see if you can turn it into a gut laugh. It's an energy changer—and energy changes us and the world around us.

Allow your friends the space to feel.

Is someone hurting, excited, envious, sad? Whatever they may be experiencing, allow your friends to feel their feelings. It's AN OPPORTUNITY FOR GROWTH AND CONNECTION. Don't be afraid to let these feelings come up. At the same time, don't squash them either.

If a friend is excited about something that's happening in their life, don't rain on their parade with bad news of your own. Wait until the celebration is over to bring up your news. **If a friend is sad, don't make it your mission to cheer them up**. I've made this mistake more than a few times in my life. In a mastermind group I was a part of, we all agreed it was okay for us to celebrate with one person and cry with the next. There was no need to sugarcoat or diminish our feelings around each other. Simply being with people and meeting them where they are emotionally is one of the best ways to be a good friend.

That's what people do who love you.
They put their arms around you and
love you when you're not so lovable.
- Deb Caletti

WHEN WE'RE CONNECTED TO OTHERS, WE BECOME BETTER PEOPLE.
- RANDY PAUSCH

Ask for help when you need it.

I've always struggled with this concept. I have a superwoman complex and think I should be able to do everything on my own, without the help of others. Yet, I find myself resentful and upset when I need help and see people standing by without lending a hand. In reality, it's me who needs to speak up and share what I'm feeling and what I need.

Most people are willing to offer their help. In fact, they love to be of service. But if they don't realize you need help they'll usually remain an innocent bystander. Make a practice out of asking for help when you need it. And when others ask you for a hand, do your best to give back as well. We all love to give, but in order to give we need people to receive. Rotate being on the giving and receiving end so you can feel balanced and satisfied within your relationships.

One area where I've learned to ask for help is in the kitchen. I love to cook. I could easily cook three meals a day, but I dislike cooking and cleaning up afterward. I feel that if I cook a meal, I shouldn't have to clean it up. The rule in my house is I'll cook as long as someone else cleans.

Party with a purpose. Social gatherings show up throughout the year. Why not make it a party with a purpose? I've seen everything from New Year's celebrations in honor of a charity to a birthday roller-skating charity event. Every year, Denver's Tammy Abramovitz combines partying with a purpose at

HER BIRTHDAY "DONATE AND SKATE" EVENT. PARTYING WITH A PURPOSE MAKES GETTING TOGETHER FUN. HOW CAN YOU COMBINE AN UPCOMING CELEBRATION WITH A CAUSE FOR GOOD?

The best way to find yourself, is to lose yourself in the service of others.
- Mohandas Gandhi

Family

Our families can be a great source for creating community. This is where many people learn how to interact with others, so be a role model and a leader in your family and **make being in community a priority.**

As a result of being brought up in an Italian family, gathering together in big herds felt normal, especially when it came to eating. Food was one of the main reasons to all come together. *There are so many ways we can bond with family, but we often take our families for granted because we believe they will always be there.* Instead, create a strong family bond within your household, and bring that sense of connectedness and togetherness out into the world around you.

Honor and acknowledge each other.

Simply being appreciative and grateful for the family in your life can change your perspective and feelings of connectedness. It's all too easy to take the people closest to us for granted. Don't. Remember to honor individuality. We are all uniquely different, and while you may not understand why your aunt, brother, cousin or other family members do the things they do, it's no reason to judge them for it. Simply remember what good they bring to your life and acknowledge them for that.

I believe we all have so much good in us, yet it takes effort to recognize the good in everyone. It's much easier to fall into the trap of negativity. When you do, stop, get back to something you love about the person and let them know those good feelings you have for them.

CREATE TRADITIONS, RITUALS AND TIMES FOR BONDING.

Rituals and traditions within families are a great way to deepen that connection and sense of community.

THIS PAST CHRISTMAS I HAD A BREAKDOWN. IT'D BEEN THREE YEARS SINCE I'D BEEN WITH MY FAMILY DURING THE HOLIDAYS. I CRIED AND THEN REALIZED WHAT I WAS MISSING WERE THE RITUALS AND TRADITIONS OF WHAT MY HOLIDAYS WERE LIKE WHEN I LIVED NEAR MY FAMILY. THESE RITUALS AND TRADITIONS INCREASE OUR TIME FOR BONDING WITH EACH OTHER—THEY ALSO SOLIDIFY OUR CONNECTIONS.

Jan Haas is amazing at creating rituals for her family. They have a ritual for so many things, including the winter equinox, holidays, rites of passage and more. These rituals and traditions help us see that we belong to something greater than ourselves. They also create lasting memories that will never fade from our memory.

The joys of laughter and good times together are another way we connect in our families. Much of our time with family can become routine, so be sure to gather together for the sake of having a little fun. Be silly. Laugh. Do something adventurous, daring and out of the ordinary. How can you set up an activity for your family that goes beyond the ordinary? Perhaps you can all volunteer together, put on a play for extended members or sing together like the Von Trapp family. My family and I once went on a cruise together. It just so happened that a hurricane was brewing in the ocean, causing the boat to rock, and all of us were feeling very ill from it. We piled into my parents' cabin, thinking of ways we could avoid the seasickness, when my brother came up with a hilarious theory about lying perpendicular to the boat to avoid the rocking feeling. We all laughed together for the longest time—it's one story none of us have ever forgotten.

Have fun together.

Write a love letter.

How often do you tell the people you care most about how important they are to you and what they mean to your life? Most likely never, or rarely.

During Christmas one year, I requested that we all write down the things we loved about each of our immediate family members. Before we exchanged gifts, we all read these thoughts out loud. It was one of the most touching, heartfelt moments in our family. We were all in tears and partially in shock, as each person brought up what they loved about everyone else. Most of what was shared related to aspects that each person didn't know others appreciated about them.

I know sharing feelings doesn't come naturally for everyone, but if you can push past your comfort zone and open your heart, it's amazing what that love does for the other person.

WHEN IS THE LAST TIME YOU SAID, "I LOVE YOU?"

Dance together.

Music is a pathway to the soul and *movement* is a vehicle for getting there. *Dancing* has always been one of my most favorite movement activities. I can easily get out on the dance floor at a wedding or other event and start to **boogie**. But I often LOVE just moving and being silly in my own home as well. One of my favorite times of the year to dance and **move** to music is during the holidays. There's something about all the glittering lights and the feeling of a decorated home that makes me want to move. Flip on some music and invite your **loved ones** to dance with you. Turn off the lights if you are too embarrassed, but regardless—**JUST DANCE**.

Eat dinner at the dining room table–together. Okay, it doesn't have to be at the dining room table, but do eat together. Everyone is on their own schedules, with their own needs and demands, but eating dinner takes less than 30 minutes. In my household, I feel like it goes down in about 10 minutes.

No matter how long or short mealtime takes, eating together is a time of day for you to connect as a family. That means no cell phones, no computers, no TV. Play the game of asking, "What was the best part of your day?" and "What was the worst part of your day?" to inspire conversation. Or come up with your own questions and ways of keeping the conversation going. Perhaps make it a rule that one-word answers are not allowed at the dinner table.

LIFE IS NEVER SO BUSY THAT THERE IS NO TIME TO SERVE.
-Author Unknown

FOOD

Growing up with Italian grandparents, food was a pivotal part of our family gatherings. Like my grandmother has always known, **food brings people together**. Most of our interactions with friends and family happen over meals.

Think about where **people gather** in your home. It's almost always **in the kitchen**. FOOD IS A WAY WE NURTURE OURSELVES AND OTHERS. I've always felt more abundant during the times in my life when I am enjoying healthy, yummy foods to feed my tummy. Today, there are an estimated **925 million hungry people in the world** (according to WorldHunger.org). To me, that's an astonishing number. I can't imagine a world without proper and adequate food for survival. Knowing how important food is to a sense of connectedness and community, it's hard to imagine so many people being without.

Food is our common ground, a universal experience.
- James Beard

Provide meals to friends, family or neighbors.

Has someone close to you just had a baby, lost a family member or experienced an illness? Gather a group of friends, neighbors or community members and plan a dinner rotation schedule. When someone experiences a new beginning or a tragedy, providing a meal is a great way to ease the burden of cooking and shopping. It seems trivial, but when someone is going through a change in life, food is often one of the hardest aspects of day-to-day living to plan for. You either can't or don't want to go out to eat, venture to the grocery store or cook a meal during times of change.

I'm at a time in my life where a lot of my friends are having babies. When a new baby arrives, one friend takes the lead and coordinates a food delivery schedule. Everyone chooses a date, cooks a meal or brings food over at some point during their day and provides the family with a meal. For those friends who don't like to cook, they pick up a pizza or order take-out. It also gives everyone a chance to visit the family and the new human being that's being welcomed into the world.

> If you can't feed a hundred people, then feed just one.
> - Mother Teresa

It's not that successful people are givers; it is that givers are successful people.

- Patti Thor

Where can you share food with others?

Cook for a local shelter.

Every community is filled with local shelters that accept cooked meals. Some require that you cook on site, while other places will allow you to cook at home and bring the meal in to be served. This is **a fun way to give back with a group of friends or family members.** You can do this for Ronald McDonald houses, domestic violence shelters, rehab facilities and other places. Ask around to find what venues are in need of food and meals within your community. You just might be surprised by how big the need for food is within your neighborhood. Coordinate an event like this with your co-workers, colleagues, friends or even strangers. It's a chance to meet people in your community and offer the gift of a delicious, home-cooked meal.

Grow a community garden.

Before moving to Colorado, I didn't have a lot of exposure to gardening. I've since started a garden every year. I love watching the plants grow and being able to walk out my back door to grab what I need and make a salad or cook some vegetables for dinner.

Community gardens have also started popping up all over the country and in corporations. Companies such as PepsiCo, Google and Yahoo have all started gardens on their properties. But, you don't have to be a Fortune

500 company to start a garden. Utilize your rooftop or containers to get going.

Not only do gardens feed people, but they bring people together. Studies have shown that gardens, digging in the dirt and getting outside can reduce stress and create bonds between people.

In Denver, CO there are over 115 active community gardens in which community members can participate. Within each of these gardens, the individual members have their own plots but additionally contribute to the main flower beds. Many of the gardens have community workdays and potlucks when everyone has the opportunity to gather together.

SHARE THE FRUITS OF YOUR LABOR.

If you have room for your own garden and tending to it brings you great joy, why not partner up with other local gardeners and share the fruits (or vegetables) of your labor? One zucchini plant makes more than any one family could possibly eat. Why not split the produce from your garden with friends and other people in the community? You can grow what you're best at growing, or what you most enjoy, and let someone else grow the plants and produce they love. Then, simply swap produce throughout the harvest periods.

One of my girlfriends is a phenomenal gardener. She produces so much spinach, romaine and greens, her family can never keep up with eating all of it. This year, we've promised to swap veggies—and I can't wait!

Kids + Food = Fun

Teach children where food comes from and how to grow their own. Kids love to get their hands dirty, and it's a great opportunity to teach them about the healthy foods that are grown from the earth.

My goddaughter, Addison, was over during the time of my tomato harvest when my cherry tomato plants were bursting with red. I couldn't keep up with eating them—they were abundant! I showed her how to pick them from the plant and eat them right from the earth.

At first she was a bit skeptical, but after she tasted one she fell in love. She loved the tomatoes so much that she cleared me out of all the ripe ones on my plants. Despite the tomatoes being a little too much for her tummy (they came right back up an hour later), she continues to ask for more tomatoes from the garden when she comes over. Her ability to walk around my garden and eat from the plants was a delight for us both.

Who doesn't love home-baked treats? Baking is the perfect opportunity to *welcome a new neighbor, celebrate an occasion or simply offer a note of thanks and gratitude.* When our new neighbor moved in across the street, I wanted him to know that he was welcome and that we were there for him. It was a busy time of year, and I just seemed to keep missing him. It was a month or two before we even introduced ourselves. I felt embarrassed that our "busy" lives had deterred us from making the effort. When I got a chance, I baked one of my favorite cakes and walked it over to make a more formal introduction.

We also gave our neighbor a welcome card and put our names on it. I realized **most people don't remember names** and feel too embarrassed to ask again, so by providing a card, he had all of our contact information at his fingertips. Make it easy on people when you can. Another great way to help others remember is to restate your name each time you see them until you are sure they know it.

A cake anyone can bake!

Pistachio Chocolate Chip Bundt Cake

1 Yellow Cake Mix
1 Package Pistachio Pudding Mix
4 Eggs
1 Cup Sour Cream
½ Cup Oil
1.5 Cups Chocolate Chips (semi-sweet)

Combine all ingredients well
and pour into greased Bundt pan.
Bake at 350 according to cake mix box instructions
(about 40-45 mins).
Let cool and then turn pan over.
Cake should fall out.
Serve (or give away).

It's always a hit.

BAKE SALES AREN'T JUST FOR SCHOOLS. IN FACT, BAKE SALES ARE A GREAT WAY TO RAISE FUNDS FOR A GOOD CAUSE. DO YOU HAVE A CAUSE YOU CARE ABOUT? IS SOMEONE YOU KNOW IN NEED? ARE YOU LOOKING FOR A WAY TO CONTRIBUTE? BAKE SALES ARE THE PERFECT WAY TO RAISE EXTRA FUNDS FOR SOMEONE OR SOMETHING IMPORTANT. YOU CAN EASILY TAKE DONATED BAKED GOODS FROM FRIENDS, FAMILY AND COMMUNITY MEMBERS AND AS YOU SELL THE TREATS DONATE THE PROCEEDS.

ORGANIZE
A BAKE $ALE.

I recently read a story about a group of women who got together for a bake sale to raise funds for a friend with cancer. There's no better way to use food than as a way to give back! A friend of mine told me that when her husband was recovering from open-heart surgery and unable to work or draw his salary, fellow employees sponsored bake sales and provided their family with all the monies raised. She and her family were extremely grateful for the financial and emotional support these efforts provided.

Holidays...
and Other Special Occasions

Holidays provide **a special time for us to think about other people.** The MAJORITY of focus on the holidays takes place around Christmas, Hanukkah and New Year's. It's when most people are thinking about giving back to others, but there are many other opportunities to give back when it comes to holidays and special occasions beyond December.

In fact, many non-profits have more help than they can handle during that time of year. Keep on giving during December if you already do, but consider how you can also incorporate some other holidays into your community building.

Invite someone new to your holiday celebration.

After moving to a new state where I didn't have extended family, I saw the importance of people opening up during their holidays and inviting others along. I've had my share of "misfit" holidays since moving to Colorado, at times celebrating Thanksgiving and Christmas with anyone who didn't have a place to go.

If you hear of someone who is homeless for the holidays, invite them into your home for a family meal. While it may not be the norm, the simple offer and gesture is enough to remind the person they are not alone, most especially when you consider how lonely people can feel during the holiday season.

Give
Receive

Give the gifts you love to receive the most. Gifts are for giving. Do you have a holiday you love? Are there certain treats you love to receive? If so, treat other people to those same indulgences.

For Easter, a group of girlfriends got together and made Easter baskets for the children at a women's domestic violence shelter. They also made baskets for the women. This is an example of one way to pass along gifts to others who may not have the luxuries that you do. This can be done with almost any holiday, from giving candy-filled cards on Valentine's Day to providing BBQ supplies and picnic gear for an outdoor-inspired holiday.

There have been so many men and women who risked their lives for us, and yet once they are back to living and working among us, they hardly receive the recognition they deserve.

Honor

My brother served in the Iraq war when it first began in 2003. It was a terribly scary time for our family. Ever since, I've never looked at a vet (young or old) in the same way. One time while walking through the Atlanta airport, a group of people holding signs cheered for our military personnel as they were being transported through the airport. I immediately choked up in tears. It means so much when our military come home safe, and we must never forget this. How can you honor a vet? Sending letters, care packages or even attending local events dedicated to their service are all things you can do to honor a vet.

During the Cold War, particularly the 60s and 70s, our service men and women didn't go through airports in uniform. The DOD ordered them to wear civilian clothes so as not to encourage demonstrations and riots. When they came home they were not welcomed. They were shunned or worse.

Congress has voted repeatedly to honor and recognize the Cold War veterans, but the DOD can't afford it and "does not recognize non-combat activity." So Cold War Salute is stirring individual Americans to say "thank you" personally. It is a project to thank those veterans who were never shown respect for their service to our country by shaking their hand, giving them a proper salute and presenting them with the U.S. Cold War Commemorative Medal. www.ColdWarSalute.com is the organizing site where any American can find a way to help make a difference for these four generations of **undervalued veterans.**

Conversation
Conversation
Conversation

"Reach out and touch someone"
- AT&T Tagline, Circa 1980

Conversation is an art which starts in the heart.

Conversation is one of my favorite activities. I've always felt there's nothing more rewarding than a deep, intimate conversation with someone, especially the kind of conversation where you walk away wondering how you even got started.

My uncle's wife was really good at this. She knew exactly how to draw a conversation out of someone. I'd often walk away wondering, how and why did I just share all that?! But now I know—it's about connection and trust. People open up when they feel safe.

Not all conversations and interactions with people will immediately be deep and juicy, but even your quick interactions with others can have meaning. To be a good conversationalist, we need to instill a sense of safety and trust into the people we speak with. We can do this by being compassionate, listening fully and with empathy. It's also important to let go of judgment or any need to control or dominate the conversation or to "fix" the other person.

Talk to a stranger. This could be anyone—someone you meet at the grocery store, while walking down the street or through a chance encounter. You never know whom you are going to meet.

One of the deliberate habits I practice is to talk to retail clerks when I check out at the grocery store. That means I get off my phone, or at least put it on hold for a minute, make eye contact and ask them sincerely how their day is going. I also like to joke about something whenever appropriate. They seem to really appreciate a customer with a sense of humor. You'll notice some people respond right away while others don't know what to do since they aren't used to being treated like a human being.

Recently, while checking out at a large retailer, I did my usual, "How's your day going today?" routine. I asked this a few times with no response from the clerk. I felt a little irritated by his lack of engagement. Why wasn't he responding to me? Here I was talking to him and he wasn't even acknowledging me. This is likely the exact way retail clerks feel all day long—invisible. Then I noticed the tag on his shirt: "Hearing Impaired." I stopped and smiled to myself. Here I was making judgments about why he hadn't responded to me, only to realize he couldn't hear me. When he handed me my bags I gave him a big smile, with an inward smile at my own ignorance, and mouthed "thank you" as clear as I could. We often take conversation for granted, but seeing him was a reminder not to take for granted our ability to hear another person when they speak to us.

> **When strangers start acting like neighbors... communities are reinvigorated.**
> – Ralph Nader

Too often we underestimate the power of a touch, a smile, a kind word, a listening ear, an honest compliment, or the smallest act of caring, all of which have the potential to turn a life around.

- Leo Buscaglia

Smile. A smile goes a long way. Don't walk with your head down, even when you are in a hurry. A simple smile can change someone's day. Try it. Even in just one place where you go today—the grocery store, the mall, at work—keep your head held high and smile. Show your teeth, give a real grin.

I've often been touted as a person with a BIG smile. And it's true. In high school I was referred to as "the girl with the Kool-Aid smile." I show both top and bottom teeth when I smile fully, and I notice when I'm smiling other people smile too. A smile is contagious. Even when people don't have anything to smile about, the majority of people will smile back. As an added benefit, this reminds people that we all matter, we are being seen and we are not invisible. When someone takes a moment to look at you and smile, it reminds you of your own presence. Go ahead, remind someone of their presence as well.

WHEN YOU ASK A QUESTION, LISTEN TO THE ANSWER. GETTING "OKAY" AS THE RESPONSE TO "HOW ARE YOU DOING?" LIKELY MEANS SOMETHING IS HAPPENING IN THAT PERSON'S LIFE. DON'T ASK HOW SOMEONE IS DOING IF YOU DON'T WANT TO REALLY KNOW. AMERICANS HAVE MADE THE GREETING OF, "HOW ARE YOU?" AN AUTOMATIC RESPONSE WITH THE SAME MEANING AS THE WORD "HELLO." IN REALITY, MOST PEOPLE AREN'T REALLY ASKING THE QUESTION AND LOOKING FOR A SINCERE ANSWER.

If you mean hello, say it. If you want to know how someone is, ask the question in a way that invites a deeper, more truthful response. Beyond greetings, also listen to the answers people give you, noting their tone and body language. Practice asking better follow-up questions to offer the opportunity for their honest replies.

I'VE OFTEN SAID IF YOU AREN'T GETTING THE ANSWERS YOU WANT, YOU'RE PROBABLY ASKING THE WRONG QUESTIONS. TRY REWORDING YOUR QUESTIONS. ASK OPEN-ENDED ONES. FOR INSTANCE, INSTEAD OF, "DID YOU DO ANYTHING FUN THIS SUMMER?" ASK, "WHAT FUN THINGS DID YOU DO THIS SUMMER?" THIS SIMPLE SHIFT WILL LEAD TO MORE EXHILARATING CONVERSATIONS.

And, if you ask a question that leads to an unexpected answer, allow the person to work through the conversation. If they are experiencing pain or sadness, give them the space to do that. A good conversationalist often doesn't need to converse, but rather IS present to the other person with a fully open heart and mind.

JUST BE

Dig deeper and ask someone about their life. What's their story? Who are they? Where did they grow up? What's their background? History? Passions? Hopes? Dreams? People love to talk about themselves, and when they find someone who will listen, even for a few moments, they'll never forget the interaction they had with you.

> It was impossible to get a conversation going, everybody was talking too much.
> – Yogi Berra

People have a strong desire to be heard. When you give a person the chance to release some of their story out into the world, they gain an opportunity for their own growth and awareness. Come with a playful sense of curiosity about people and you just might be surprised at what you find.

YOUR PRESENCE IS YOUR POPULARITY.

Be totally present. Give someone a few minutes of your undivided attention and you'll find that your relationships deepen. It's rare we spend even a few minutes a day talking to someone without multi-tasking. Drop your other tasks and pay attention. Be in the present moment with them. This will do wonders for your personal relationships.

If you can't give someone your full attention, ask if you can talk later once you complete what's in front of you, so you can be fully present with them. They will appreciate it, even if their initial reaction is unfavorable. Children and the people closest to us only need a few moments of undivided attention daily to feel they matter.

CAN YOU RECALL THE COLOR OF THE EYES OF THE PEOPLE YOU INTERACT WITH THE MOST?

Make eye contact.

Eye contact often gets lost in the times in which we live. We are texting while walking, cooking dinner while talking about the day, looking at our computer as we participate in a meeting. Taking a few moments to look deeply into someone's eyes will show you a window to their soul. Have you ever noticed how people have trouble keeping their eyes locked with someone else's, even someone close to them? Try maintaining eye contact with your loved ones and even strangers. It's our habit to look away when someone's eyes meet our own, but resist the impulse to do so. Stop, look and smile.

Compassion hurts.
When you feel connected to everything,
you also feel responsible for everything.
And you cannot turn away.
Your destiny is bound with the destinies of others.

You must either learn to carry the Universe or be crushed by it. You must grow strong enough to love the world, yet empty enough to sit down at the same table with its worst horrors.
- Andrew Boyd

I STRONGLY BELIEVE WHEN WE INFUSE LOVE AND ENCOURAGE SELF-ESTEEM IN CHILDREN, WE SET THE TONE FOR A FUTURE WITH HEALTHY, CONNECTED AND EMPATHETIC ADULTS. When we focus on developing the well-being of children, we can shift their perspectives of the world to eliminate poverty, hunger and other ailments that plague our planet. Children are simply little people soaking up all that is in their environment. Why not fill their environment with everything they need to grow into healthy, striving and thriving adults?

When I worked in my first business, a youth theatre franchise, I hosted a summer day camp. There were over twenty kids in my week-long drama camp, and on the very first day I knew I was in trouble. Two brothers came in together and they were more than a handful. By the second day, I knew that if I didn't change my perspective

Children

about these boys and shift what was happening within them, they'd ruin the camp for all the kids who were in attendance.

Remembering my philosophy that the only thing children need is love, I mustered up all the love in my heart and poured it into those little boys. Within one afternoon, they shifted. One even curled up in my lap soaking in my love during movie time. They weren't perfect for the rest of the week, but they significantly improved. I saw then the amazing power of love and how receptive children are to it. As adults, we just need to be brave enough to give it, even when it's challenging.

GET DOWN ON THEIR LEVEL. ALL DAY LONG CHILDREN LOOK UP TO ADULTS WHO TOWER OVER THEM. CHILDREN ARE LITTLE PEOPLE. WHEN YOU GET DOWN ON THEIR LEVEL, THEY'LL SHOW YOU A LOT MORE RESPECT. THINK OF A TOWERING BOSS OR ANOTHER PERSON IN POWER. HOW DOES IT FEEL WHEN THEY USE THEIR PHYSICAL PRESENCE OVER YOU? IT LIKELY CREATES AN IMMEDIATE DISCONNECT. IT'S A CLASSIC POWER POSITION. WHEN WE CAN GET DOWN ON THE SAME LEVEL PHYSICALLY, CHILDREN OPEN UP MORE EASILY AND WILLINGLY. THEY WILL ALSO PAY MORE ATTENTION TO YOU AND WHAT YOU SAY TO THEM.

> The soul is healed by being with children.
> - Fyodor Dostevsky

ALLOW YOUR INNER CHILD TO COME OUT AND PLAY. Have you ever seen the magical way children admire an adult who can act like a kid? They know it's not easy. They can tell we live in a "grown-up" world. But, if you can allow your inner child to come out for just a few minutes, to be silly, act like a monkey and roll around on the ground, you'll have them laughing their little hearts off.

Once, when I was playing with my nephew and a few other kids, I activated my drama skills and created "secret spy missions." In the beach condo where we were staying, we found a few fun things to use as costumes. A hairband with cotton swabs turned into a makeshift eye-patch, and we used other household items as a part of our spy-gear. Soon, we were sneaking around the building acting like spies. We ran low and close to the ground, hid behind concrete posts and found ourselves giggling, breathless and having an amazing time together. The kids that night thought what we had done was extremely "cool"—it was one of the highlights of our time together. Other kids I've played that game with since have never forgotten it either.

That's the real trouble with the world, too many people grow up.

- Walt Disney

Remember life isn't serious unless we make it that way. We may believe that a clean house and being on time really matter, but if you dig deep, it's the quality of time we spend with the ones we love that will mean something to us on the day we leave this planet. Assess what's truly important. You can give a child love and undivided attention or focus on what's only a temporary pain: leaving a bed unmade, the dirty shirt soaking and arriving a few minutes late.

When my boyfriend's family visited us from Indiana one summer, his two nieces were restless while the adults all needed some time to relax. Instead of joining the adults, I remembered not to take life too seriously and decided to hang out with the kids. I opened our storage box of Halloween costumes and dressed the kids and myself in wigs, jewelry and other silly items. We made a sign that said "Peace & Love—$1" and stood near the busy highway. We then walked up to the local ice cream store, still in our costumes, and sat outside eating our ice cream cones. I laughed the whole way there and back.

Nothing you do for a child is ever wasted.
- Garrison Keillor

Acknowledge a child for doing something right. There's power in acknowledging a child for doing good. The majority of children only receive attention when they do something wrong, which causes them to act out even more to seek attention.

As adults, we may feel that when we reprimand a child, the attention is perceived as negative and they'll want to avoid it in the future, but to a child attention is attention, no matter how you slice it. Whether it's sharing their candy, playing quietly or doing what you've asked, make it a point to notice children when they're doing these things. When you give attention for doing something right, you'll notice a significant shift in the behavior of a child who has been used to receiving negative-based attention.

Give love. All children need is love. I believe if every child in this world received unconditional love while growing up, they would be well-adjusted, happy, CONFIDENT adults. What would it take to love the children in your life unconditionally? Yours and others.

> Children are likely to live up to what you believe in them.
> - Lady Bird Johnson

SWAP
babysitting

Whether you're a two-parent household or a single parent, making time for everything in your life can be a challenge. A great example of community is when parents come together to share child-rearing responsibilities. Kid-swaps are a great way to give parents a break, whether to recharge, get projects done around the house or go on a date and reconnect!

Find a parent or couple to partner with and create a rotating schedule. One set of friends I know created a point system. Every time they watched another person's child, they received a point. Later, they were able to "cash" in their points when they needed a sitter for their own child. It was a great way to ensure the swaps were even for all the parents participating.

> No act of kindness, however small, is ever wasted.
> - Aesop

> **TRULY WONDERFUL THE MIND OF A CHILD IS.**
> **- YODA**

Teach children empathy. Children are very receptive to what is happening in the world around them, especially when we give them a chance to participate and see first-hand the situations of others. Empathy is a learned skill, and the sooner we teach children to give back and participate in our community and society, the greater chance they will develop empathy and compassion for all human beings, animals and the planet.

I recently volunteered with a group of friends at a shelter for single parents. We served dinner to the parents and their children. A few of our friends' children came with us as well—they wanted to help. I was amazed at how great the kids were. They knew they were there to volunteer and help others. When I told them they could get in line for food, they replied with, "Thanks, but we want to make sure everyone else has eaten first." Wow! I was impressed. On the way home, one of the girls (age 10) said, "It just shows how selfish we can be sometimes, but actually we are really blessed." I think that says it all.

Animals

My mother worked at a veterinarian's office throughout my entire childhood. She passed on her love of animals to me and my siblings. We occasionally heard about some of the animals that came into their office, but mostly I think my mom loved her work because she connected on a different level with animals.

As human beings, I feel it is our responsibility to protect three important elements of our existence: nature, children and animals. These are the three living beings that cannot protect themselves.

ADOPT AN ANIMAL. CONTRIBUTING BACK TO THE COMMUNITY INCLUDES BEING A RESPONSIBLE PET OWNER. THAT MEANS GETTING YOUR DOGS AND CATS PROPERLY SPAYED OR NEUTERED. IT MEANS FEEDING THEM AND GIVING THEM THE LOVE AND ATTENTION THEY NEED AND DESERVE.

At 23, I lived a few hours away from my hometown. Without any pets, the house felt empty. I knew I wanted a furry friend to share my love with, so I ventured down to the local humane society. That's where I found my first cat, Tucher. He was lovable, and I was thrilled to have him in my life. When I realized what an amazing cat he was, I started volunteering at that same humane society. I spent all my free time there, between going to school full-time and working. I couldn't wait to go into the shelter to help clean the cat cages, play with the kitties waiting for adoption and even clean out their mite-infested ears. It wasn't long before another young cat came into the shelter that I also wanted to adopt. As soon as I laid eyes on her, I immediately put her on hold. I had to wait for the three-day waiting period to clear, in case someone came in to claim her. Luckily, no one did and now Sophie has also been with me for over ten years.

Both dogs and cats can bring much love into your home. If you love animals but aren't sure about the commitment they require, spend some time volunteering at an animal shelter to get your furry-friend-fix and learn more about what it would take to make such a commitment.

OUR BELOVED PETS.
HOW THEY TOUCH OUR SOUL.
HOW THEY LIFT OUR SPIRITS.
FOR THEY ARE MORE THAN A PET,
THEY ARE A TEACHER ON OUR JOURNEY.

If you already have a wonderful pet, share your animal with others. Beyond service dogs that ultimately end up with their new owners, you can share your wonderful pet with others in need. Most hospitals, retirement homes and rehabilitation centers accept well-behaved pets into their facilities to spread their love and attention. People who love animals are thrilled to see a four-legged friend after they've been cooped up for a while without any pet contact.

SAVE AN ANIMAL. While visiting home one year, I was out in the backyard when a puppy around six months old strolled up to the fence. I approached the dog and immediately noticed that its collar was deeply embedded into its skin. The dog was bleeding badly and smelled of rotting flesh. As I left the yard and moved toward the dog, it started to run away.

I couldn't let it get too far because I knew most people would not make the effort to approach it. After quite a bit of coercion, I was finally able to capture the dog. We loaded him into the car and drove to the nearest emergency vet hospital (since it was well beyond normal office hours by then). When we arrived at the vet, I let them know that I didn't live in the state any longer and I couldn't afford the services this dog would require. Emergency vets have a strict policy: payment is due before services are rendered and they don't take care of strays. I was in tears. This dog was sweet and deserved a chance, but I knew I couldn't give it to him.

I sat in the exam room and waited for the doctor to come back, scared of what they would tell me. When the doctor entered the exam room, she told me she understood this was not my dog and knew I didn't have a way to keep it or get it back to Colorado. They agreed to take care of it and give it the proper treatment it needed, and I would not be billed for the services. I immediately broke down and cried. That hospital saved this young dog and gave it a fighting chance.

It is not only for what we do that we are held responsible, but also for what we do not do.
- Moliere

TRANSPO

Our wheels and modes of transportation provide another way for us to give back. Planes, trains and automobiles are how we travel and get from Point A to Point B.

In my early 20's, as I was driving around an Orlando neighborhood, a pedestrian walked into the street to cross the road at the exact same moment I was making a right turn. My little Honda Civic ran over her foot, and I was alarmed by what had happened. I immediately stopped to check on her—she was in pain but forgiving. She asked me for a ride to where she needed to go, which was about 15 minutes away. To this day, I wonder what that encounter was really about. Perhaps she just needed a ride and it was all divinely inspired. Either way, I was able to be of service to her that day. However you get around, you can be a source of service too.

RTATION

Stop and help someone when they are having car trouble. With everyone trying to get to their next destination in a hurry, most travelers start honking and react with irritation when a person is stalled. Most likely, a stalled car means the individual is experiencing trouble with their vehicle. **Instead of getting upset, be the person who helps.** If safe to do so, assist them and move their car to the side of the road. Call for assistance or if you know how to help with the problem, such as change a flat tire, go ahead and lend them a hand.

One night I drove home late after I'd worked at our family restaurant in Florida. It was dark and traffic was extremely heavy on I-4, the main interstate in Orlando. Because traffic was moving slowly, my car overheated. I pulled over and contemplated my options. I knew I was only about 1.5 miles from my exit and I just lived a few blocks from there. (This was before cell phones.) **I made a decision to get out and walk.** It seemed like a better choice than waiting out the night.

As I started to walk, a truck driver rolled down his passenger side window and yelled out, "You need a ride?" My heart leapt. *A ride from a truck driver?* Perhaps I should take my chances and walk. "No thanks," I replied. "Come on," he said. "I've got a wife and daughters and I wouldn't want them walking out here alone. Besides, where am I going to take you in this traffic?" I don't know exactly what made me do it, but I figured he made sense. I hopped in the truck and prayed I'd be seen by my family again—alive! As my exit neared, he slowed to the side of the road and I got out, safe and sound.

When I look back, I now believe he was protecting me, and I am forever grateful for that ride. Although my mother was sourly disappointed I'd taken a ride from a trucker, I followed my gut on this one, and my gut turned out to be correct.

In another instance, my business partner Lisa was driving along when she got a flat tire. She pulled off to the side of the road. Two young men and a girl, who were on their way to a bar, stopped to help her. **They spent over an hour changing her tire and refused to accept any money for their good deed.** These are exactly the kinds of stories that make my heart sing.

OFFER A RIDE. If you've got the time and the wheels, offer a ride to someone in need. The seniors in our community need to be taken to the doctor, the grocery store and the pharmacy to take care of their basic needs. A lot of these people no longer have a car or are no longer capable to drive one on their own. And among these, not all have family or live near a relative who can provide help.

As people age, they often lack proper and adequate self-care, mostly because they are missing the resources (i.e., transportation) to ensure their well-being. My grandmother, who is now 83, has a woman drive her around for her errands every couple of weeks. This woman takes her to the grocery store, the bank and anywhere else she needs to go. I'm grateful that people are willing to spend their time taking care of people in need, such as my grandmother.

It is one of the most beautiful compensations of this life that no man can sincerely try to help another without helping himself.
- Ralph Waldo Emerson

Donate your old car.
Over the last few decades, donating our old cars has become increasingly popular. If you have a car that has reached its peak for your purposes, consider donating it to a charity. There are tax benefits to donating your car, so speak to your accountant about this first. If it makes sense for you, this is another way to give back.

There are people, pets and children that need to travel. Funds aren't always available for their travels, but with the help of frequent flier miles, traveling by air can become accessible. For example, one local Colorado non-profit, My Opportunity Foundation, which provides life skills training to teen orphans in Kazakhstan, regularly takes trips to the country in order to donate their time and resources to the children who will eventually age out of the orphanage system. They are always in need of funds for flights or frequent flier mile donations.

Many business travelers have more miles than they know what to do with and other people have miles that are going to expire or that they'll never use. If that's the case for you, consider donating your miles to a worthy cause.

DONATE
your
MILES

SHIP GOODS FOR GOOD REASONS.

Without ever running a non-profit, I never considered all the things it takes to make one work. My friend Karen Loucks Rinedollar started a non-profit, Project Linus. This organization makes homemade blankets for children in need. Many of these blankets have been shipped around the world, but shipping doesn't happen for free. Karen brought this to my attention and explained how people can give back by helping goods get from one place to another.

For example, are you moving across the country or to another state and have extra room in your moving truck? Or do you work for a company that makes large deliveries or freight shipments and can store other goods within the boxes or trucks? If so, consider partnering with a non-profit for a one-time stop or an ongoing partnership. In the case of Project Linus, people help blankets get to faraway places and into the hands of sometimes very ill and severely traumatized children.

Around Town

As I've said previously, the average person knows approximately 250 people. On an average day, you potentially pass more than 250 people while driving on the road, shopping at the grocery store, filling up your car with gas, running an errand or encountering other people in your office building. All of these moments are opportunities to be of service. Similar to performing random acts of kindness, when you are out and about in your daily routine, you can easily give back. It's the beauty of being connected and being in service at the same time. Service doesn't have to be a big deal either. In fact, many times it's the small things that make the biggest difference in someone's life.

> We were born to unite with our fellow men, and to join in community with the human race.
> - Cicero

Be silly in public places. I truly think this is the purpose of flash mobs—to get people to stop, take notice and watch something unfold before their eyes. While you don't need to coordinate a dance, what else could you do to get people to smile, to help people feel connected or to bring light to a person's day?

As a teenager, a group of girlfriends and I used to head to the busy street near our homes and stand by the road waving at the cars that passed by. It was such fun for us, and we got a lot of waves and honks in return. The other day I saw a homeless man with a sign that said, "Dog and wife abducted by aliens, need ransom money." I laughed out loud at that one.

Denver local, Avram Gonzales, created what he calls InspirAction, where he took a challenge to do something different every day for a year. During that year he had a day of silence, a day with no shoes and many other fun and often silly experiences. He also created many videos documenting his experience, which was a great way for him to stay connected and create a ripple effect of inspired action.

Learn people's names. Do you have places you visit frequently, such as the dry cleaners, your favorite restaurant or a local store? If so, start to learn the people's names who work there. I once heard a quote from Dale Carnegie that stated, *"The greatest sound anyone can hear is the sound of their name."* Make it a practice to learn people's names and use them. And if you've forgotten someone's name, say so right away. People are very forgiving when it comes to restating their name. They'd rather you ask than have you pretend you know it and get caught in a pickle when you aren't able to recall it for an introduction.

It's okay to forget, but practice remembering. I've made it a practice to get better at remembering names. When I see someone I haven't seen in a while and remember their name, it leaves quite an impression on them. Recalling someone's name makes them feel important—which is what remembering names is all about.

Holding the door for someone is likely one of the easiest, simplest and most old-fashioned ways we can serve, but it truly is an act of service. Whenever you go through a door, see if there is someone close by for whom you can pause and hold the door.

I've often held doors for men coming and going, and I can't tell you how surprised most of them are. I believe we all deserve the courtesy of someone holding the door for us, whether we're male or female. While many of the men push me through and end up holding it for me, the gesture is still very much appreciated. Be sure to especially look for opportunities to hold the door for mothers, disabled individuals and seniors. A lot of doors today have the automatic button, but many still do not.

You can also carry someone's groceries, another way to offer a helping hand. In actuality, this is about lending a helping hand when you see a person who could use the help. Groceries seem to be the most traditional expression for lending a hand, but there are plenty of ways to offer help, from someone unloading a truck, carrying a box or even moving a piece of furniture. Even within your own household, how can you give a helping hand to someone?

Personally, I love it when my boyfriend comes out of the house to help me unload the groceries. Growing up, whenever we heard my mom return from the grocery store, we all ran outside to grab a few bags. We were partially just curious to see what she bought, but it was still a gesture of help regardless of the intent.

offer a helping hand.

There can be no **vulnerability** without **risk**; there can be no **community** without **vulnerability**; there can be no **peace**, and ultimately no **life**, without **community**.
- M. Scott Peck

LET SOMEONE GO AHEAD OF YOU. We've all seen people who are in an obvious hurry. We've all been that person who is in a hurry —we need to quickly get on the road, make a turn or get out of the line to get somewhere. Why not let someone go ahead and get in line in front of you? When offered, people are very surprised by this, and many will not even accept, but the offer is appreciated.

Recently, I was in line at the grocery store and the person behind me had two things. I had a basketful of items. I offered that they go ahead, and they took me up on it. When I got up to the cashier, the clerk said to me, "That was really nice of you. You can't imagine how many people won't do that." The clerk's observation was enough for me to make a habit out of stepping back in line to allow someone else to go ahead of me.

Going

There are unlimited amounts of resources available to us within our communities. Sometimes we don't know where to look. Sometimes we don't know who we are looking for and at other times we simply just don't even ask. Regardless of what or who you may need, or what you may offer, going local has its advantages. Not only is it fun to support local vendors, restaurants and service professionals, but every time we contribute to the local

WE ARE IN COMMUNITY EACH TIME WE FIND A PLACE WHERE WE BELONG.
- PETER F. BLOCK

community in some way, we feel more connected to those around us.

Local

That's part of why I love one of my volunteering efforts, where I facilitate conversation groups at a school for refugees who are learning English. It helps me realize how diverse our community is and how many people, whom I don't even know or come in contact with on a regular basis, are a part of the community where I live.

Be a connector.
Being a connector is similar to putting together a puzzle. It's fun when you've found a piece that fits. That's why we all love to recommend the people we love. "I had a great haircut—here's my new stylist's information." "My doctor is amazing—here's their number." Yet, connecting can go beyond service professionals. Connecting is about linking people up with the resources that could improve their lives. Whether it's helping them build their business or recommending a child care provider, when we connect others with the things they need, we see how we are all deeply connected within our community.

Sabrina Risley, the owner and founder of a local networking organization, has this mindset and skill mastered. She's an amazing connector and always seeks out opportunities to link people together. She has a relationship-builder mentality and practices what she teaches. As I believe, if you are looking for more from people, it's time to step up and give more of yourself to others.

That best portion of
a good man's life;
his little, nameless,
unremembered acts of
kindness and love.
- William Wordsworth

Get involved in a community event. Whether in your neighborhood or city, there are plenty of events that happen year-round all over the world. Perhaps you can be a volunteer or even participate. For example, if you are feeling really creative, why not create a float for your town parade? Look for different ways to be of service and get involved in your community at local events. Once they come into your awareness, you just might be surprised at how many events happen in your hometown throughout the year. This is a fun way to meet new people and give back.

SUPPORT LOCAL SHOPS AND BUSINESSES. WHENEVER YOU CAN, SUPPORT LOCAL. IN TODAY'S WORLD WE CAN GET ALMOST ANY PRODUCT WE NEED ONLINE, BUT BETTER YET, WE CAN GET A LOT OF OUR PRODUCTS LOCALLY. ONE OF MY FAVORITE OUTINGS DURING THE SUMMERTIME IS VISITING THE FARMERS MARKETS, WHICH ARE FILLED WITH LOCAL FOODS AND VENDORS. YOU'LL FIND SOME OF THE GREATEST PRODUCTS AND GOODS AT THESE EVENTS, AND YOU ARE NOT ONLY GETTING GREAT ITEMS, BUT YOU ARE ALSO SUPPORTING THE PEOPLE WITHIN YOUR COMMUNITY. LOOK FOR ALL TYPES OF LOCAL PRODUCTS, FROM FOOD TO CLOTHING TO WINE. SOME OF MY FAVORITE LOCAL ITEMS ARE HANDMADE SOAPS (SUN TURTLE NATURALS - MADE IN LOUISVILLE, CO) AND THESE DELICIOUS LITTLE CARAMELS I CAN ONLY FIND AT THE MARKET, AND OH YEAH, I CAN'T FORGET ABOUT THE LOCAL FOOD TRUCKS AS WELL! LOCALLY INSPIRED FOOD AND FLAVORS ON WHEELS - YUM!

THE REVERSE IS ALSO TRUE FOR BUSINESSES. IF YOU ARE A LOCAL BUSINESS, GET INVOLVED IN YOUR LOCAL COMMUNITY. I WAS IN A LOCAL GROCER AWHILE BACK AND THE STORE WAS EMPTY. IT WAS AS IF THE COMMUNITY HAD ABANDONED IT, DESPITE ITS GOOD FOOD. THE OWNER SAID TO ME, "THE PEOPLE IN THIS COMMUNITY JUST DON'T CARE. THEY ONLY CARE ABOUT PRICE." SILENTLY I ASKED MYSELF WHAT HE WAS DOING TO GIVE BACK AND CREATE COMMUNITY IN HIS SMALL NEIGHBORHOOD, BUT I ALREADY KNEW THE ANSWER. IT'S A TWO-WAY STREET. IF YOU ARE A LOCAL BUSINESS, DO WHAT YOU CAN TO GET ENGAGED IN YOUR COMMUNITY. IT WILL COME BACK TO YOU TENFOLD. MY FRIEND SUE HYATT, THE AUTHOR OF **STRATEGY FOR GOOD**, IS A MASTER AT LEVERAGING COMMUNITY PARTNERSHIPS WITH BUSINESSES SO IT'S A WIN-WIN FOR ALL.

I'm a big advocate of literacy, but not just for children—adults too. IN THE U.S., IT'S BEEN REPORTED THAT ONE IN SEVEN ADULTS CANNOT READ, APPROXIMATELY 14% OF THE POPULATION. That seems like too many if you ask me. You can volunteer in ESL (English as Second Language) classes or visit your local library and read to a child. Either way, you are helping someone become a more productive, happier member of society by learning to read.

For a time, I used to read stories to children at our local community gardens. It was great fun to watch the children as I read to them. Some would request that I read something over and over again, while others could barely sit still long enough to hear one story. Regardless, I'm a lover of books, and I find such joy in reading that literacy has become a cause I care about deeply.

TEACH SOMEONE TO READ.

You give but little when you give of your possessions. It is when you give of yourself that you truly give.
- Kahlil Gibran

Offer your services or skills to others.

Are you skilled at computers? Are you an incredible tailor? What are you really good at and how could you share those skills with others? There are plenty of ways to serve by using your talents. For instance, many non-profits need volunteers with expertise in marketing, administration and other office-type tasks. If you have a skill you can donate, get in touch with a non-profit you are passionate about and help by donating your human-power.

Donna Mazzitelli, my friend and editor, loves to write. Recently, she became acquainted with a local non-profit organization that provides toys and personal care items to underprivileged children who live in the local community. The non-profit was in need of someone to write its weekly blog and monthly newsletter. She now volunteers her time and writes throughout the month on their behalf. It's gratifying for her and greatly appreciated by the organization to have someone take care of a task that didn't come easily to the founder or other volunteer staff.

Beyond non-profits, there are likely people in your community who could also benefit from your services. So, when you think about doing good, consider those who are nearby. Quite possibly they aren't speaking up for help.

My parents' neighbor is an elderly woman with a prosthetic leg. My parents often help her with household chores and various tasks because they know she can't do them all alone. In return, their neighbor frequently drops by with lots of baked goodies to say thank you. My own grandmother has a neighbor who helps her out in the same way, and our family is grateful for their care and attention.

Create art with friends, family and in your community. Art is a great way to celebrate community. One way to come together with art is through creating community murals.

During high school, I was heavily involved in student government. One of our tasks during our senior year was to create a mural that represented the school. Many of us came in on the weekends and painted a large mural on the wall in the cafeteria. It was complete with our mascot and other objects that represented the school.

Once we are able to let our guard down and remove our own self-judgment about our creative abilities, both kids and adults can find great joy and community when creating art together. Where or how can you contribute a mural to your community? Is there perhaps an oppressed neighborhood or downtown area where you could honor an important contributor to your city?

Everybody can be great...because anybody can serve. You don't have to have a college degree to serve. You don't have to make your subject and verb agree to serve. You only need a heart full of grace. A soul generated by love.
- Martin Luther King, Jr.

A man has made at least a start on discovering the meaning of human life when he plants shade trees under which he knows full well he will never sit.
- D. Elton Trueblood

Sing for seniors. Seniors are a subgroup of our population that could benefit greatly from a little extra care. There are plenty of ways to give back when it comes to seniors. One of the more simple ways is to show up at a local retirement facility or nursing home and offer your time and attention.

My first job while in high school was waitressing at a retirement home. I learned so much about the senior population during that time, and I also made some great friends. I only worked at the job for one year, but the people there made a lasting impression that has never left me.

Think of the things you can do for seniors—from singing, to performing a play, to entertaining them in some other way. Or perhaps you can offer a class or lead a craft. Don't forget about the people who came before us, and ensure their last years truly are golden by offering a little time, love and attention.

BE A CONSCIOUS CONSUMER. Have you ever considered where the products you purchase actually come from? The people who produce them? The materials from which they are made? The shipping and transportation involved? If you think about everything that goes into any product you purchase and consume, you might be amazed—or alarmed—at all the hidden "costs" involved in its creation.

When we practice being a conscious consumer, however, we take time to consider what, where and how we buy. It's about looking at the whole picture. Perhaps a product costs less, but if the product has a damaging effect on the environment, the people and the economy where it's produced, is the cost really less? And is that cost really worth it?

What if instead we took the time to understand where every product we purchased came from? What if we understood the impact of that product on the planet? What if we considered not only the product itself, but the outer packaging that is often created in big, bright ways to appeal to our sense of need? And how about if we also took a look at its recyclability or reusability before we purchased it? How might taking these factors into consideration impact our consumer choices? Let's rethink how, what and why we buy.

One of my favorite brands is Patagonia. They are a socially responsible company and produce high quality active wear. Their clothing is made of recycled material, and you can be assured that when you make a purchase there, the profits are being put to good use.

I'm a nature junkie. If I could throw a mattress in the woods and live there, I would. There's something about being in nature that makes me feel CONNECTED. Ironically, it's when I spend time alone in nature that I often feel the most in touch with all that is happening in the world. It's a way for me to quiet my mind and get out of my head—where I believe our true source of disconnection comes from. Nature gives us the space to reconnect with ourselves, so we can then go out into the world and be more connected to others. Don't discount the magical power of being alone and being in nature.

Nature

Where can you get more access to nature? Do you have a local park, a trail or even a garden nearby? If so, make time to get outside and enjoy the natural beauty Mother Earth so lovingly shares with us. When you do, you'll feel more connected to the world around you. Also, bring the outdoors inside with you. Find a favorite place, take a picture of it, print and frame it so you can see yourself there when you aren't able to be outdoors.

When you go outdoors, simply breathe in the fresh air and take in the sunshine. I probably don't need to tell you that a daily healthy dose of Vitamin D can do wonders for your mood

Get out and experience the joys of nature.

and immune system. But just in case you didn't know, this is a reminder to get outside. I'm saddened by how many people live their lives indoors—I'm guilty of this at times myself. Earth is a playground, meant to be loved, adored and most of all explored. I can't tell you how many days I've said to myself, "Wow, I didn't even get outside today!" Let's make a habit of getting outside for even one minute to stop and breathe in the fresh air. You're worth it!

DIG IN THE DIRT

Did you play in a sandbox or dig in the dirt as a child? I remember building sand castles on the beach, digging for worms in our yard and even playing with Matchbox cars on our long dirt driveway in Florida. We'd come inside the house covered with dirt. When I was a young girl, we had horses and lived on a few acres of land. There was a sense of freedom about being able to roam around among the orange groves and wander through a big open space. Digging in the dirt brings me back to that childhood sense of wonder. That's why every spring I get so excited about filling our pots with soil and flowers, planting our garden and just getting dirty.

One year, when spring had arrived and nature was in full bloom, I did snow angels in the grass. Try that sometime. Your friends will think you're crazy, but I promise it'll bring much joy to your day.

Your deepest roots are in nature. No matter who you are, where you live, or what kind of life you lead, you remain irrevocably linked with the rest of creation.
- Charles Cook

ORGANIZE A GROUP OUTING. There's a plethora of opportunity awaiting you in the great outdoors. What kinds of community activities can you coordinate outdoors where you live—a walk in the woods, a snowshoe trip, a stroll along the beach? Even a play date at the park signifies getting outside and bringing people together. When weather permits, take your gatherings outdoors.

Nature is not only all that is visible to the eye – it also includes the inner pictures of the soul.
– Edvard Munch

GO CAMPING WITH FRIENDS. My parents like to RV. Personally, I love sleeping in a tent, but I realize not everyone feels the same way. Regardless of whether camping is your style or not, getting together for an outdoor overnight with friends or family will guarantee a fun adventure.

I've seen many children respond favorably to these outings. They enjoy sleeping in the woods and being outside just as much, if not more, than adults, so don't let kids, pets or anything else keep you from experiencing a night under the stars every so often. And, by the way, an RV counts for that too.

BOND OVER A BONFIRE. The warmth of the flames forces people to get closer together. Have you ever noticed how we huddle around the heat? Whether you build a bonfire (in a safe space) out of natural wood, or even a fire pit in your backyard, people begin to let their guard down a little. It's as though the flames of the fire break down barriers of what we hold onto in the light of day. Conversations go deeper, people are more open and you'll likely not even notice time passing while being mesmerized by one of nature's strongest forces.

WALK A 5K, RUN A MARATHON, BIKE, SNOWSHOE OR SWIM FOR A CAUSE. Whatever sport feeds your fancy, there's an occasion built around it waiting for those who want to get physical for a cause they care about. There are a lot of races that combine a sport, charity and fun. Go ahead, register for one today.

For example, in Colorado we have the Romp to Stomp, a snowshoe adventure where people dress in costume for the Susan G. Komen Foundation; the Llama Rama, where you race with a llama for organ donation; the Furry Scurry, where dogs and people run for the Humane Society; and the Scream Scram, a Halloween costume run for the Boys and Girls Club. If you don't have an event like this near you, find your favorite charity and see how you can team up to have fun, get outside, move and support a cause in your community.

Go out, go out I beg of you.
And taste the beauty
of the wild. Behold the
miracle of the earth
with all the wonder
of a child.
– Edna Jaques

ENVIRONMENT

Our planet is one of the most spectacular and amazing miracles. It produces just the right amount of oxygen, water and plant life. It houses millions of species of plants, animals and insects. When I think of the planet earth, I am in a state of gratitude that we get to live in a place of such beauty. Think about all the amazing places that inhabit our world, from the Grand Canyon to Mount Everest.

As human beings, with our own conscious evolution, we have a responsibility to take care of the earth's natural resources and to protect the land and the environment. There are many things that we can do to protect the earth, and as we become more conscious about the planet in which we live, it creates an even greater sense of community, connectedness and belonging, especially when we remember how we are really living in one spectacular place, under one roof, with shared resources.

**REDUCE
REUSE
RECYCLE**

How can we limit our consumption to ensure there will be enough resources for future generations? What would it take to recycle all material goods into something that we can reuse? You can reduce your carbon footprint by taking small steps to reduce, reuse and recycle. For instance, trade in plastic water bottles for a permanent water bottle. These now come in a variety of shapes, sizes, colors and styles so you can easily make a personal statement with your water bottle. Also, bring your own grocery bags to the store—not only does this save on plastic use, the reusable grocery bags store more and actually make transporting groceries easier.

I could easily go on about all the ways to reduce, reuse and recycle, but remember that even small steps make a big difference to the environment. Recycling all materials properly can help a great deal. From now on, consider how you can reuse and pass along other household items that you would normally think about tossing away.

In today's economy, we are seeing more creative businesses emerge that are utilizing these principles. One such store is Revampt, which creates household furnishings from repurposed materials, including everything from bike wheels to dilapidated machinery. It just goes to show that everything desires a second chance.

Pick up trash and litter.

The world is our home. It is not our trash can. While here in the U.S., people pride themselves on keeping clean communities, we still see large amounts of trash and junk along roadsides. I'm amazed at how many people can unconsciously toss trash out their car windows, as if it magically finds its way into the proper disposable bins.

When I visited the country of Belize, I was amazed at how much trash washed along the shores of the beach. It broke my heart to see the ocean cluttered with litter, and due to island living, the trash had nowhere to go. I understand it's a part of the culture, but when we get back to respecting the earth and feeling connected to it, we can see how it is our responsibility to pick up after ourselves. It only takes a few seconds and a little extra effort to dispose of our waste.

My stepfather is one man who is completely passionate about cleaning up trash and litter. I have to admit, I've been embarrassed by his passion at times, but now I commend him for not caring what other people think and instead taking a stand for something. Whenever we are walking outside, he'll stop and scoop up whatever trash he sees. He goes for walks that are two to three hours long, just because he picks up trash along the way. He not only ends up with bags of trash, he also separates the cans and recycles them. Here's a man who has found his own way to give back and to protect the beautiful planet Earth.

Ride your bike, walk or carpool. There are over 1 billion cars on the road worldwide. Consider the amount of consumption of gas and natural resources for every car, along with pollution, traffic and congestion. Instead of always traveling by automobile, find ways to travel by bike or on foot. Personally, I love riding my bike around town or walking to do my errands. Even if you just walked to the store or rode your bike to drop off your dry cleaning once a month, imagine what would be possible if everyone did this? How much could we reduce our carbon footprint if we took small steps that added up? Many people worry they don't have enough "time" to be green or to be more environmentally conscious, but time is all we have. If we don't do it now, if we don't make changes in this moment, we affect every generation that comes after us. Don't let time be an excuse. Think about all the people who will come after us, from your children, to their children and their children.

> Think of bicycles as rideable art that can just about save the world.
> - Grant Peterson

If you must take your car and drive, find a person to carpool with. Cities are making carpooling easier with convenient parking lots and other public transportation means. Carpool when you can, drive when you must.

Biking can be fun. When you are planning your next vacation or family outing, look to see how you can bike your way around town. In Denver, they now have 52 bike stations scattered across the city with over 500 bikes that both locals and visitors can use at any time. It's a great way to get around the city and visit local attractions, while being more environmentally friendly.

COMPOSTING.

Composting is something you can do year-round, and it's a win-win activity to participate in. Composting is a great way to turn waste (organic preferably) into healthy food for your plants. It keeps yard and food waste, which make up about a quarter of what we throw away in the U.S., out of landfills. Composted material is much richer food for your plants than chemical fertilizers, which actually deplete soil. Adding compost to your soil also provides it with lots of nutrients and improves the soil's pH levels.

For more information on getting started, go to www.composting101.com or talk to your local garden shop.

Charity

At five years old, I tagged along with my dad when he went to work. Our family owned a fast-food, fried chicken restaurant, and my dad was the store manager. It was in a less affluent neighborhood, and homeless people often lingered around the restaurants to get leftover food.

One evening, as we started to pull away from the back of the building, we noticed a homeless man digging through the dumpster, looking for scraps. My father stopped the car. He yelled for the man to stop. Then he proceeded to go inside the restaurant. We didn't know what he was doing. I thought he was going inside to call the police. Instead, my dad came out with a box of fried chicken and handed it to the man. I knew then that helping others was something that was a part of our responsibility as human beings.

Years later, when my brother opened his own restaurant, he also fed the homeless by giving them odd jobs they could help with. The homeless people knew they could work for food by picking up litter around the building or doing other tasks my brother needed done.

Act as if what you do makes a difference. It does.
- William James

FIND A WAY TO SERVE.
We typically view
charity in two ways—
volunteering and making donations.
Both are perfect expressions
of being of service.
But if you don't have extra money
or you don't have time,
there are still plenty of things you can do.
Be creative.
You'll find a way to serve.

Notice the homeless. Did you know homeless people say they feel invisible? Our society overlooks them. They rarely receive eye contact. People look around them. It's as if they don't even exist. Do you know what's it like to feel invisible? What would it take for you to smile at someone who lived on the streets, no matter how scared it made you feel? One day when I practiced this, a homeless man looked me back in the eyes and gave me a "thumbs up." It made me smile. That was all I could give him in the moment, but at least it was something, and most importantly I gave him the gift of honoring his humanity.

> If you want others to be happy, practice compassion. If you want to be happy, practice compassion.
> - Dalai Lama

How wonderful it is that nobody need wait a single moment before starting to improve the world.
- Anne Frank

Donate your skills

What skill do you have to donate? Beyond regular volunteering, such as building a house for Habitat for Humanity or at a special fundraising event, most non-profits and charities need individuals to fill positions within the organization. For example, are you a social media whiz? Perhaps you can use your skills to volunteer for a favorite charity. Are you good at marketing, administration or fundraising? Why not go into the office for a few hours a month and support the causes you care about?

SUPPORT A CAUSE OR CREATE A GROUP FOR A CAUSE. How can you support a cause you believe in? There's a plethora of causes we can support that appeal to each and every one of us who wants to get involved. You can choose anything from animals, nature, poverty, abuse, pollution, children, education and more. Many charities need help with special events, fundraising, ongoing administration and hands-on volunteering. Find a cause you care about and then find the best way to get involved. Through the years I've volunteered my time at the humane society, where I adopted my two cats, assisted in equine therapy for disabled children, read books to children, mentored an at-risk youth and led conversation groups for refugees trying to learn English. Those are just some of the things I've done, and all included causes I care about. When we give back to those around us, we tend to value our own significance in this world.

People often come together to support a cause. This can be anything from a group of friends, concerned parents or colleagues and co-workers. This is how M.A.D.D. (Mothers Against Drunk Driving) and so many other groups started. If you find you have a cause you are passionate about, why not rally together other local, national or international supporters and lead a charge for change?

I am only one,
but I am one.
I cannot do
everything,
but I can do
something.
And I will not let
what I cannot do
interfere with what
I can do.
- Edward Everett Hale

Become an advocate for something you believe in.

Who or what can you become an advocate for? Perhaps you have a politician you stand behind and believe in. Maybe you've initiated a new bill to be passed by your local government or you want to fight for another person's rights. All of these are worthy causes for you to advocate. Perhaps you've noticed that a new stoplight needs to be installed to eliminate the high number of accidents on a nearby corner or you're willing to go door-to-door to get a petition signed. Any of these can be worthy causes worth fighting for.

Nobody can do everything, but everyone can do something.
- Author Unknown

Believe in Someone

Really great people make you feel that you, too, can become great.
- Mark Twain

Sadly, so many of us grow up without truly feeling as though anyone believes in us. Least of all, we often don't believe in ourselves. Yet, self-confidence and self-efficacy are the roots of success, livelihood and happiness.

What would it take to create a world where we all believed in everyone around us? How often have we placed judgment on others because of their background, skin color, past actions or religion? How have we kept others small so that we ourselves could feel better? Instead, let's see how we can stop doubting and start believing in those around us.

Every little action we take, every word we say, every thought we think has an effect on others. When we take responsibility for our thoughts, beliefs and actions, and turn them into something positive and productive, the world inevitably changes.

It seems as though some people are born with confidence, while others work their entire life to achieve it. I believe we can help facilitate confidence in others by truly seeing their greatness, even when they can't see it for themselves.

Recently, while I was in Florida visiting my family, I had the chance to play basketball with my nephew. He had developed a new love for the sport, so we did some bonding on the court. He shot a few free throws and missed. He was deeply disappointed and even went so far as to say, "I suck!" Being the type of person I am, I wouldn't and couldn't allow such negative self-talk. He mumbled something about never being able to make free throws and that it was never going to happen.

I made him stop, visualize the throw, see it going into the basket and hear the silent "whoosh" of a net ball. I stood there patiently with him as we practiced. He missed the first few, but I encouraged him not to give up and assured him that

PASS ALONG CONFIDENCE AND HELP SOMEONE BELIEVE IN THEIR OWN SELF-WORTH.

he could in fact make those baskets. In less than five minutes he made his first one. Then he challenged himself to make two in a row. In less than fifteen minutes, he'd completed that challenge, but it wasn't without having to overcome a lot of self-doubt. Yet, together we stood there and held the vision. Each time, he visualized the shot before he threw the ball.

When he finally got two in a row he beamed with excitement. He ran to me, jumping up and down and threw his arms around me. We celebrated his success. It was amazing. Sometimes confidence comes with patience, and sometimes we need a supportive, loving hand to see what we can accomplish. Be that person for others.

BE A ROLE MODEL/MENTOR. What if we all had just one person in our lives who could be a positive, stable role model for how our lives could be? How could that influence or change the destiny of another person? People don't know what they don't know. The role of a mentor is to not only encourage, inspire and provide support to another, but also to let the mentee know, or remind them, of what's possible for their life.

I believe that every person is born with talent.
- Maya Angelou

It reminds me of the tale about a woman who chopped off a third of a ham every time she cooked it. When someone asked her why she did it, she responded, "It's what my mother did." As she investigated further, she asked her mother why she chopped off a part of the ham, and her mother replied, "It's what my mother did." Then, they both asked the grandmother why she had always chopped off part of a ham before she cooked it, and she replied, "Because I didn't have a pan big enough."

We all get CAUGHT UP IN PATTERNS, REPEATING WHAT WE LEARNED for no other reason than because we were shown that way or because our family and peers believed it to be true. While our families bring significant value to our lives, the habits and behaviors that have been passed down may not always serve us. When you become a role model for someone, whether a child in need or a co-worker, YOU GIVE THEM PERMISSION TO SEE THINGS DIFFERENTLY.

Worship, meditate and celebrate together.

Community is often found within a church or place of worship, but I believe we can practice the habits of fellowship, meditation and celebration in any space where we come together.

One family I know gets up every morning to meditate together. It's a way for them to connect, not only with each other, but to something greater. I've also attended a local spiritual center for their noon meditations. It provides a way to ground myself and set the stage to remain centered throughout my day. It's also a fantastic way to come together with people in the community for something good.

We saw other amazing examples of this when the "Occupy Wall Street" movement was in full effect and groups of people came together to meditate. You can come together at any time, with anyone you choose, to pray, meditate or even celebrate. It's the energy of coming together that's important.

Start a prayer circle.

When a person falls ill, is struggling personally or financially, or is simply going through a challenging period, perhaps it's time to coordinate a prayer circle. Typically these circles are not done in person, but are rather a showering of love, thoughts and prayers throughout a specific time period.

If someone you know is in need of love and support, gather as many people as possible and choose a specific time of day to all come together to offer this energetic healing. Remember, it doesn't have to be in person. Everyone can make their offering at the same time or you can have an ongoing circle of support starting with one person and then moving on to the next. Above all, hold this person in the most amazing light imaginable. Whether you pray, meditate or send loving thoughts, just send all the good you can in their direction.

Stand up for someone.

There are times in our life when we all need someone to take a stand for us, whether the situation involves kids who are up against another kid or a bully, or a friend struggling with a difficult spouse or partner, or some other circumstance. There are thousands of scenarios where we can take a stand for someone else. I'd like to suggest that first we empower those people to stand up for themselves, but there are times when they cannot. There are times when they are so disempowered that someone else needs to step in and offer assistance.

I'll never forget the time as a teenager when we planned a family outing to the Daytona Beach Boardwalk. It was only about 30 minutes from our family home. We were heading there to grab dinner and play video games. As we approached the boardwalk, we saw a crowd gathered together. My step-father immediately took notice.

As we got closer, we saw that two men were fighting. In actuality, it was one man fighting. The other was already beaten badly and on the ground. The man standing continued to throw

> Be kind whenever possible.
> It is always possible.
> - Dalai Lama

punches at the man lying on the ground. My step-father jumped in and broke up the fight. None of us could believe it. My mom shrieked for him to stop, but adrenaline had kicked in. He was able to quickly stop the fight and then yelled for someone to call an ambulance. He turned on the crowd and shouted, "You all are just standing here?! Get out of here. NOW!" (My step-father could be an intense man, especially when he saw something that wasn't right.) The crowd quickly dispersed. That was one of the most courageous things I've ever seen in my life, and I'll never forget what he did for that stranger when no one else would.

You see everything is about belief, whatever we believe rules our existence, rules our life.
- Don Miguel Ruiz

MindFULLness

There are now 7 billion people on the planet. When I think of that number, I'm in absolute amazement. Especially when you consider some of what that means—there are 7 billion different human thoughts vibrating and happening at the exact same time. With the various styles of living and culture, each person is having a unique experience in any given moment. Everything about their life is different than everyone else's, down to their perceptions and experiences. Yet, we are all deeply connected, bonded by the human spirit.

In the context of this topic, I speak of the practice of mindfulness as being in the present moment and expanding our connection to those around us. I find that when I am being mindful, I feel more deeply connected to the planet, to people and to my life's work. When I am mindful I feel as though I belong, as though I can make an impact and make a difference for others. To me, those are the most important aspects of being a living being, but I realize I must stay mindful and present to these feelings in order to activate that energy within me. It's all too easy to get caught up in the daily grind and whiz through our days, realizing later that we never took a moment to be fully present.

THINK OF OTHERS OFTEN. The simple act of becoming more mindful includes thinking of others. I have many friends who are exceptional at this. They are the type of people who know what you need and even make an effort to be of service without being asked.

One day I was feeling under the weather. I had been hit hard with a cold and was complaining to my friend, Jan, that I was sick. She emailed me and said, "Don't eat lunch, I'll bring you some." Within a few hours, she was over with homemade chicken soup and we ate lunch together. It was such a great treat.

Beyond food, there's still plenty we can do when we think of others. **Simply being present with a person when they are speaking of something difficult is a gift.** Not judging them. Not needing to speak. All of these things include thinking of the other person. Find individual and unique ways to express this gift of mindfulness.

Write a thank you letter.

Unlike a traditional thank you letter that comes when someone does something for you, write a letter thanking someone for their presence in your life. Let them know what they've contributed to your life, how they've inspired you, influenced you or what you admire most about them. Put this letter in an envelope and mail it with a stamp—no emails please. The recipient will get to hold on to this written message forever, to run it through their hands and remember their contributions whenever they want or need it for reassurance, unlike what happens when we get an email, which likely stays locked up in our computer.

To be mindfully engaged is the most natural, creative state we can be in.
– Ellen Langler

TAKE A MOMENT TO REACH OUT TO ANYONE IN YOUR LIFE.

Phone, text, email. I can't tell you how many times I've thought to myself, I should reach out to so-and-so. Tasks, to-do's and obligations take over and then I'm reminded again. Reach out to so-and-so. When you get these messages or inspirations to reach out to someone, do it.

A few weeks ago I was feeling particularly frustrated. I was in one of those moods where I felt like I wasn't making progress fast enough and I was having a bit of a pity party, when my phone rang. On the other end was Donna, who said, "I just had this feeling I should call you right now." I burst into tears. Just knowing someone had sensed I needed a loving ear and acted on it was miraculous.

You never know what is going to be on the other end when you reach out to someone. Perhaps it's a normal, everyday conversation, but maybe you might just heal a wounded heart, inspire a smile or even take away a burden. Who can you reach out to today?

Take a picture of yourself with the following message attached to the photo: "You are amazing!"

Images affect people. It's an extra step, whether you send it through your camera phone or you actually print out a digital photo and pop it in the mail. Think of all the fun or inspiring messages you can send with a word or a phrase.

CampExperience is a charity-inspired women's retreat held each year in Colorado. As a part of the fifth anniversary event, we honored the founder with a compilation of photos. It turned into a four-minute video of many people showering her with love and appreciation. The video was such a treat, not only for the founder, but for everyone who participated. People were excited and couldn't wait to see the finished product showing how everyone came together to offer this to her.

To take this one step further, why not make a video message to share with someone? With the ease of technology at our fingertips, sending personal messages has never been easier. It's a gift they can keep forever and replay over and over again.

*If instead of a gem,
or even a flower,
we should cast the gift
of a loving thought into
the heart of a friend,
that would be giving
as the angels give.*
- George MacDonald

Turn off your vices...I mean devices. Turn off your TV, computer and cell phone. There are so many distractions to give into at any moment, but what if we just stopped using them or at least paused them long enough to take notice of what is right in front of us at any given moment?

One day, in a Washington, D.C. metro station, a man played a violin for about 45 minutes. During that time, it was estimated that 1,100 people passed him. What took place that

DAY WAS AN EXPERIMENT TO SEE IF PEOPLE WERE PAYING ATTENTION AND WHETHER THEY WOULD NOTICE WHAT WAS IN FRONT OF THEM. THE MUSICIAN WAS A MAN NAMED JOSHUA BELL, ONE OF THE WORLD'S GREATEST VIOLINISTS, PLAYING ON A 3.5 MILLION DOLLAR INSTRUMENT. OUT OF ALL THE PEOPLE WHO PASSED HIM BY, ONLY SIX PEOPLE STOPPED TO LISTEN AND HE RECEIVED $32 IN DONATIONS. THIS STORY HELPS US REMEMBER THAT WHEN WE ARE BUSY AND PREOCCUPIED, WE DON'T RECOGNIZE WHAT IS RIGHT THERE—IN FRONT OF US.

We are already one.
But we imagine
that we are not.
And what we have
to recover
is our original unity.
What we have to be
is what we are.
– Thomas Merton

Honor cultures, connectedness and past generations. What if we lived in a world that completely celebrated our diversity, yet embraced how we were all uniquely connected? What would that look like? It's a world that I envision and hope to see come together during my lifetime. We are all human beings having a human experience on this planet. There is no separateness, no division. Yes, we may have various skin colors and socio-economic backgrounds. We even have different traditions, values and beliefs—but we are all connected by the human spirit.

How can you honor and celebrate diversity? Have you attended a holiday or cultural tradition within your community? Do you still see life as divided? Become a global citizen and find your connection to other cultures. When we experience a sense of connectedness to other cultures, we honor that culture for where they are, we do not ask them to change or to be "like us." Instead, we are loving and accepting, much the same way a parent is to a child.

You can also feel that sense of connectedness by looking at our past generations and celebrating the people who came before us. We still have much to learn from our ancestors. Let's never forget they were here before us.

SERVICE

I'd be remiss to talk about service and community-building without putting emphasis on the importance of self-care. There's a reason flight attendants tell parents to take the oxygen mask first before giving it to their child. If we aren't taking care of ourselves and setting an example of that for others, we aren't doing anyone any good. The more we take care of ourselves, the more we can pass along love, compassion, acceptance and the many other good and positive feelings in our world.

However, when we are tired, burned out and bitter about not having our own time, we serve no one. Taking time for myself has been a huge lesson in my own growth, and it's now something I strongly believe in and encourage in others. When you do what's right for you, it's always doing what's right for others.

Taking time for yourself and practicing proper self-care can look different to different people. For me, doing anything crafty, spending time outside or giving myself permission to have fun and play are all activities that feed my spirit and leave me feeling rejuvenated.

TO THE SELF

In dealing with those who are
undergoing great suffering, if you
feel "burnout" setting in, if you feel
demoralized and exhausted, it is best,
for the sake of everyone, to withdraw
and restore yourself. The point is to
have a long-term perspective.
- Dalai Lama

In our culture, we often feel the need to keep doing. "What needs to get done," seems like a never-ending message to be attentive to everyone else's needs. Somewhere along the line, downtime became devalued and sometimes even deemed as being lazy. However, our brains and our bodies are not meant to run from sunup to sundown seven days a week. Take time to do nothing. Whether nothing means reading a book, star gazing or strolling down the sidewalk, "nothing" is good for the soul. Take a hot bath, pause, sit in silence—these are all things you can "not" do in order to recharge.

Allow yourself time to do nothing.

Spend time with people who reflect your greatness.

In life, we get to choose our friends and who we spend time with. Make a commitment to surround yourself with people who value and appreciate you, lift you higher and make you want to be a better person.

I notice when I'm around the people who lift me up, my energy is higher and I can see an endless stream of possibilities for my life. When I am around other people who can only see the negative and are generally unhappy, I have a harder time staying in my happy place. When I find myself acting in ways in which I remember, "this is not who I am," I limit my time with that person or people. It's about saying yes to YOU, so you can really serve the world and make a bigger impact.

Practice self-acceptance.

The more we love, accept and forgive ourselves, the more we will love, accept and forgive others. There's power in loving yourself. Never forget what an amazing, remarkable, powerful person you really are. It's your truth. Wherever you are is okay, and who you are is absolutely perfect.

This is last, but not least.

Pass this book along. If you want to be an agent for change, then help others to become empowered, compassionate, service-driven members of your community. You can do this by passing along a copy of this book to someone else. They'll thank you for it, and so will I!

The 101 Ways to Be of

Neighborhood
1. Shovel your neighbor's sidewalk or clear off their car
2. Grab your neighbor's newspaper or other packages when they are out of town and stow them away until they get back home
3. Create a neighborhood contact list
4. Start a neighborhood watch
5. Plan a neighborhood block party. Spearhead an annual neighborhood event
6. Build a bonfire, light a fire pit and create a neighborhood drum circle
7. Invite your neighbors over to your house for dinner, appetizers or game night
8. Share resources
9. Host a community garage sale
10. Gather your gently-used goods and donate them to a local shelter

At Work
11. Lift each other up
12. Be inclusive
13. Speak kind words
14. Offer support
15. Coordinate community involvement
16. Get physical
17. Company potlucks
18. Giveaway tables

Friends
19. Pray, send love, keep high in thoughts
20. Be vulnerable and authentic
21. Laugh
22. Allow your friends the space to feel
23. Ask for help when you need it
24. Party with a purpose

Family
25. Honor and acknowledge
26. Create traditions and rituals
27. Have fun
28. Write a love letter
29. Dance together
30. Eat dinner together

Service & Create Community

Food
31. Provide meals to friends/neighbors
32. Cook for a shelter
33. Grow a community garden
34. Share the fruits of your labor
35. Teach children where food comes from
36. Baked goods. Baked treats as sweets for others
37. Organize a bake sale

Holidays
38. Invite someone new
39. Give gifts
40. Honor a vet

Conversation
41. Talk to a stranger
42. Smile
43. Ask someone about their life
44. Be present
45. Make eye contact

Children
46. Get down on their level
47. Allow your inner child to come out and play
48. Don't take life too seriously
49. Acknowledge a child for doing something right
50. Give love
51. Swap babysitting
52. Teach empathy

Animals
53. Adopt an animal
54. Share your animal
55. Save an animal

Transportation
56. Help someone with car trouble
57. Offer a ride
58. Donate your old car
59. Donate your miles
60. Ship goods for good reasons

Around Town
61. Be silly
62. Learn people's names
63. Do a good deed. Hold the door/groceries
64. Let someone go ahead of you

Continued...

Going Local
65. Be a connector
66. Community event
67. Support local shops and businesses
68. Teach someone to read
69. Offer your skills to others
70. Create art in your community
71. Sing for seniors
72. Be a conscious consumer

Nature
73. Get out in nature Breathe in the fresh air
74. Dig in the dirt
75. Organize a group outing
76. Go camping with friends
77. Bond over a campfire
78. Walk a 5k, run a marathon

Environment
79. Recycle
80. Pick up trash/litter
81. Ride your bike
82. Compost

Charity
83. Find a way to serve
84. Notice the homeless
85. Donate your skills
86. Support a cause
87. Become an advocate
88. Lead a charge/Create a group for a cause

Believe in Someone
89. Pass along confidence
90. Be a role model/mentor
91. Worship/celebrate
92. Prayer circle
93. Stand up for someone

MindFULLness
94. Think of others often
95. Write a thank you letter
96. Reach out to someone in your life
97. Send a picture message
98. Turn off your devices
99. Honor cultures, connectedness and past generations

Service to the Self
100. Allow time for nothing
101. Spend time with people who reflect your greatness
102. Practice self-acceptance

acknowledgments

This book wouldn't be possible without my amazing support system. My gratitude goes out to all who were involved from start to finish.

Special thanks to Donna Mazzitelli, the Word Heartiste, for working her artistry on this book, for encouraging me to share more and go deeper. Thanks to Jess Bonasso for helping me hone my message and ideas. To Jan Haas, Lisa Shultz, Izzy Driscoll and Julio Blanco for your encouraging support. To Amanda Solomon for sharing your cake recipe.

To my sister, Kimberly, for your feedback and skillful eye. To my family, who has provided many examples of how to serve.

And to Rob, for your belief in me.
Thank you all.

about the author

Andrea Costantine witnessed her first example of compassionate service early in life, when at five years old she saw her father give a box of fried chicken to a homeless man digging in the dumpster behind their family restaurant. As a teen, the only thing that kept her out of trouble (and her grades decent), was being involved in student government, where she contributed to both her school and the local community. As an adult, Andrea has volunteered for various non-profits, including the animal shelter where she adopted her two cats, literacy efforts, children's services and local events.

Today, she finds herself inspiring others to make a difference in the world where we live. Andrea's adoration for the human spirit is expressed through her public speaking, workshops, and books where she leads others to embrace a service mindset and live with compassion, so that together we can change the world.

Professionally, Andrea has a Master's Degree in Human Services, is certified in life coaching and is a creative visionary entrepreneur at heart.

She resides in Denver, CO with her enjoyable other and two cats.

Andrea can be reached through her website at www.andreacostantine.com.

*Connected is available for businesses,
nonprofits and educators.
For special pricing and printing options,
email info@andreacostantine.com
or visit www.theconnectedbook.com.*

CPSIA information can be obtained
at www.ICGtesting.com
Printed in the USA
FFOW03n1339180414
4885FF